The Imaginary Invalid by Molière

Le Malade Imaginaire

Jean-Baptiste Poquelin is better known to us by his stage name of Molière. He was born in Paris, to a prosperous well-to-do family on 15th January 1622.

In 1631, his father purchased from the court of Louis XIII the posts of "valet of the King's chamber and keeper of carpets and upholstery" which Molière assumed in 1641. The benefits included only three months' work per annum for which he was paid 300 livres and also provided a number of lucrative contracts.

However in June 1643, at 21, Molière abandoned this for his first love; a career on the stage. He partnered with the actress Madeleine Béjart, to found the Illustre Théâtre at a cost of 630 livres. Unfortunately despite their enthusiasm, effort and ambition the troupe went bankrupt in 1645.

Molière and Madeleine now began again and spent the next dozen years touring the provincial circuit. His journey back to the sacred land of Parisian theatres was slow but by 1658 he performed in front of the King at the Louvre.

From this point Molière both wrote and acted in a large number of productions that caused both outrage and applause. His many attacks on social conventions, the church, hypocrisy and other areas whilst also writing a large number of comedies, farces, tragicomedies, comédie-ballets are the stuff of legend.

'Tartuffe', 'The Misanthrope', 'The Miser' and 'The School for Wives' are but some of his classics.

His death was as dramatic as his life. Molière suffered from pulmonary tuberculosis. One evening he collapsed on stage in a fit of coughing and haemorrhaging while performing in the last play he'd written, in which, ironically, he was playing the hypochondriac Argan, in 'The Imaginary Invalid'.

Molière insisted on completing his performance.

Afterwards he collapsed again with another, larger haemorrhage and was taken home. Priests were sent for to administer the last rites. Two priests refused to visit. A third arrived too late. On 17th February 1673, Jean-Baptiste Poquelin, forever to be known as Molière, was pronounced dead in Paris. He was 51.

Index of Contents

SCENE XXIII
MOLIÈRE – A SHORT BIOGRAPHY
MOLIÈRE – A CONCISE BIBLIOGRAPHY

DRAMATIS PERSONAE
ARGAN, an imaginary invalid
BÉLINE, second wife to ARGAN
ANGÉLIQUE, daughter to ARGAN, in love with CLÉANTE
LOUISON, ARGAN'S young daughter, sister to ANGÉLIQUE
BÉRALDE, brother to ARGAN
CLÉANTE, lover to ANGÉLIQUE
MR. DIAFOIRUS, a physician
THOMAS DIAFOIRUS, his son, in love with ANGÉLIQUE
MR. PURGON, physician to ARGAN
MR. FLEURANT, an apothecary
MR. DE BONNEFOI, a notary
TOINETTE, maid-servant to ARGAN

THE IMAGINARY INVALID (LE MALADE IMAGINAIRE)

ACT I

SCENE I

ARGAN sitting at a table, adding up his apothecary's bill with counters.

ARGAN
Three and two make five, and five make ten, and ten make twenty. "Item, on the 24th, a small, insinuative clyster, preparative and gentle, to soften, moisten, and refresh the bowels of Mr. Argan." What I like about Mr. Fleurant, my apothecary, is that his bills are always civil. "The bowels of Mr. Argan." All the same, Mr. Fleurant, it is not enough to be civil, you must also be reasonable, and not plunder sick people. Thirty sous for a clyster! I have already told you, with all due respect to you, that elsewhere you have only charged me twenty sous; and twenty sous, in the language of apothecaries, means only ten sous. Here they are, these ten sous. "Item, on the said day, a good detergent clyster, compounded of double catholicon rhubarb, honey of roses, and other ingredients, according to the prescription, to scour, work, and clear out the bowels of Mr. Argan, thirty sons." With your leave, ten sous. "Item, on the said day, in the evening, a julep, hepatic, soporiferous, and somniferous, intended to promote the sleep of Mr. Argan, thirty-five sous." I do not complain of that, for it made me sleep very well. Ten, fifteen, sixteen, and seventeen sous six deniers. "Item, on the 25th, a good purgative and corroborative mixture, composed of fresh cassia with Levantine senna and other ingredients, according to the prescription of Mr. Purgon, to expel Mr. Argan's bile, four francs." You are joking, Mr. Fleurant; you must learn to be reasonable with patients; Mr. Purgon never ordered you to put four francs. Tut! put three francs, if you please. Twenty; thirty sous.[1] "Item, on the said day, a dose, anodyne and astringent, to make Mr. Argan sleep, thirty sous." Ten sous, Mr. Fleurant. "Item, on the 26th, a

carminative clyster to cure the flatulence of Mr. Argan, thirty sous." "Item, the clyster repeated in the evening, as above, thirty sous." Ten sous, Mr. Fleurant. "Item, on the 27th, a good mixture composed for the purpose of driving out the bad humours of Mr. Argan, three francs." Good; twenty and thirty sous; I am glad that you are reasonable. "Item, on the 28th, a dose of clarified and edulcorated whey, to soften, lenify, temper, and refresh the blood of Mr. Argan, twenty sous." Good; ten sous. "Item, a potion, cordial and preservative, composed of twelve grains of bezoar, syrup of citrons and pomegranates, and other ingredients, according to the prescription, five francs." Ah! Mr. Fleurant, gently, if you please; if you go on like that, no one will wish to be unwell. Be satisfied with four francs. Twenty, forty sous. Three and two are five, and five are ten, and ten are twenty. Sixty-three francs four sous six deniers. So that during this month I have taken one, two, three, four, five, six, seven, eight mixtures, and one, two, three, four, five, six, seven, eight, nine, ten, eleven, twelve clysters; and last month there were twelve mixtures and twenty clysters. I am not astonished, therefore, that I am not so well this month as last. I shall speak to Mr. Purgon about it, so that he may set the matter right. Come, let all this be taken away.

[He sees that no one comes, and that he is alone.

Nobody. It's no use, I am always left alone; there's no way of keeping them here.

[He rings a hand-bell.

They don't hear, and my bell doesn't make enough noise.

[He rings again.

No one.

[He rings again.

Toinette!

[He rings again.

It's just as if I didn't ring at all. You hussy! you jade!

[He rings again.

Confound it all!

[He rings and shouts.

Deuce take you, you wretch!

SCENE II

ARGAN, TOINETTE.

TOINETTE
Coming, coming.

ARGAN
Ah! you jade, you wretch!

TOINETTE [Pretending to have knocked her head]
Bother your impatience! You hurry me so much that I have knocked my head against the window-shutter.

ARGAN [Angry]
You vixen!

TOINETTE [Interrupting **ARGAN**]
Oh!

ARGAN
There is ...

TOINETTE
Oh!

ARGAN
For the last hour I ...

TOINETTE
Oh!

ARGAN
You have left me ...

TOINETTE
Oh!

ARGAN
Be silent! you baggage, and let me scold you.

TOINETTE
Well! that's too bad after what I have done to myself.

ARGAN
You make me bawl till my throat is sore, you jade!

TOINETTE
And you, you made me break my head open; one is just as bad as the other; so, with your leave, we are quits.

ARGAN

What! you hussy....

TOINETTE
If you go on scolding me, I shall cry.

ARGAN
To leave me, you ...

TOINETTE [Again interrupting **ARGAN**]
Oh!

ARGAN
You would ...

TOINETTE [Still interrupting him]
Oh!

ARGAN
What! shall I have also to give up the pleasure of scolding her?

TOINETTE
Well, scold as much as you please; do as you like.

ARGAN
You prevent me, you hussy, by interrupting me every moment.

TOINETTE
If you have the pleasure of scolding, I surely can have that of crying. Let every one have his fancy; 'tis but right. Oh! oh!

ARGAN
I must give it up, I suppose. Take this away, take this away, you jade. Be careful to have some broth ready, for the other that I am to take soon.

TOINETTE
This Mr. Fleurant and Mr. Purgon amuse themselves finely with your body. They have a rare milch-cow in you, I must say; and I should like them to tell me what disease it is you have for them to physic you so.

ARGAN
Hold your tongue, simpleton; it is not for you to control the decrees of the faculty. Ask my daughter Angélique to come to me. I have something to tell her.

TOINETTE
Here she is, coming of her own accord; she must have guessed your thoughts.

SCENE III

ARGAN, ANGÉLIQUE, TOINETTE.

ARGAN
You come just in time; I want to speak to you.

ANGÉLIQUE
I am quite ready to hear you.

ARGAN
Wait a moment.
[To **TOINETTE**]
Give me my walking-stick; I'll come back directly.

TOINETTE
Go, Sir, go quickly; Mr. Fleurant gives us plenty to do.

SCENE IV

ANGÉLIQUE, TOINETTE.

ANGÉLIQUE
Toinette!

TOINETTE
Well! what?

ANGÉLIQUE
Look at me a little.

TOINETTE
Well, I am looking at you.

ANGÉLIQUE
Toinette!

TOINETTE
Well! what, Toinette?

ANGÉLIQUE
Don't you guess what I want to speak about?

TOINETTE
Oh! yes, I have some slight idea that you want to speak of our young lover, for it is of him we have been speaking for the last six days, and you are not well unless you mention him at every turn.

ANGÉLIQUE

Since you know what it is I want, why are you not the first to speak to me of him? and why do you not spare me the trouble of being the one to start the conversation?

TOINETTE

You don't give me time, and you are so eager that it is difficult to be beforehand with you on the subject.

ANGÉLIQUE

I acknowledge that I am never weary of speaking of him, and that my heart takes eager advantage of every moment I have to open my heart to you. But tell me, Toinette, do you blame the feelings I have towards him?

TOINETTE

I am far from doing so.

ANGÉLIQUE

Am I wrong in giving way to these sweet impressions?

TOINETTE

I don't say that you are.

ANGÉLIQUE

And would you have me insensible to the tender protestations of ardent love which he shows me?

TOINETTE

Heaven forbid!

ANGÉLIQUE

Tell me, do you not see, as I do, Something providential, some act of destiny in the unexpected adventure from which our acquaintance originated?

TOINETTE

Yes.

ANGÉLIQUE

That it is impossible to act more generously?

TOINETTE

Agreed.

ANGÉLIQUE

And that he did all this with the greatest possible grace?

TOINETTE

Oh! yes.

ANGÉLIQUE

Do you not think, Toinette, that he is very handsome?

TOINETTE
Certainly.

ANGÉLIQUE
That he has the best manners in the world?

TOINETTE
No doubt about it.

ANGÉLIQUE
That there is always something noble in what he says and what he does?

TOINETTE
Most certainly.

ANGÉLIQUE
That there never was anything more tender than all he says to me?

TOINETTE
True.

ARGAN
And that there can be nothing more painful than the restraint under which I am kept? for it prevents all sweet intercourse, and puts an end to that mutual love with which Heaven has inspired us.

TOINETTE
You are right.

ANGÉLIQUE
But, dear Toinette, tell me, do you think that he loves me as much as he says he does?

TOINETTE
Hum! That's a thing hardly to be trusted at any time. A show of love is sadly like the real thing, and I have met with very good actors in that line.

ANGÉLIQUE
Ah! Toinette, what are you saying there? Alas! judging by the manner in which he speaks, is it possible that he is not telling the truth?

TOINETTE
At any rate, you will soon be satisfied on this point, and the resolution which he says he has taken of asking you in marriage, is a sure and ready way of showing you if what he says is true or not. That is the all-sufficient proof.

ANGÉLIQUE
Ah! Toinette, if he deceives me, I shall never in all my life believe in any man.

TOINETTE
Here is your father coming back.

ARGAN, ANGÉLIQUE, TOINETTE.

ARGAN
I say, Angélique, I have a piece of news for yon which, perhaps, you did not expect. You have been asked of me in marriage. Halloa! how is that? You are smiling. It is pleasant, is it not, that word marriage? there is nothing so funny to young girls. Ah! nature! nature! So, from what I see, daughter, there is no need of my asking you if you are willing to marry.

ANGÉLIQUE
I ought to obey you in everything, father.

ARGAN
I am very glad to possess such an obedient daughter; the thing is settled then, and I have promised you.

ANGÉLIQUE
It is my duty, father, blindly to follow all you determine upon for me.

ARGAN
My wife, your mother-in-law, wanted me to make a nun of you and of your little sister Louison also. She has always been bent upon that.

TOINETTE [Aside]
The excellent creature has her reasons.

ARGAN
She would not consent to this marriage; but I carried the day, and my word is given.

TOINETTE [To **ARGAN**]
Really, I am pleased with you for that, and it is the wisest thing you ever did in your life.

ARGAN
I have not seen the person in question; but I am told that I shall be satisfied with him, and that you too will be satisfied.

ANGÉLIQUE
Most certainly, father.

ARGAN
How! have you seen him then?

ANGÉLIQUE
Since your consent to our marriage authorises me to open my heart to you, I will not hide from you that chance made us acquainted six days ago, and that the request which has been made to you is the result of the sympathy we felt for one another at first sight.

ARGAN
They did not tell me that; but I am glad of it; it is much better that things should be so. They say that he is a tall, well-made young fellow.

ANGÉLIQUE
Yes, father.

ARGAN
Of a fine build.

ANGÉLIQUE
Yes, indeed.

ARGAN
Pleasant.

ANGÉLIQUE
Certainly.

ARGAN
A good face.

ANGÉLIQUE
Very good.

ARGAN
Steady and of good family.

ANGÉLIQUE
Quite.

ARGAN
With very good manners.

ANGÉLIQUE
The best possible.

ARGAN
And speaks both Latin and Greek.

ANGÉLIQUE
Ah! that I don't know anything about.

ARGAN

And that he will in three days be made a doctor.

ANGÉLIQUE

He, father?

ARGAN

Yes; did he not tell you?

ANGÉLIQUE

No, indeed! who told you?

ARGAN

Mr. Purgon.

ANGÉLIQUE

Does Mr. Purgon know him?

ARGAN

What a question! Of course he knows him, since he is his nephew.

ANGÉLIQUE

Cléante is the nephew of Mr. Purgon?

ARGAN

What Cléante? We are speaking about him who has asked you in marriage.

ANGÉLIQUE

Yes, of course.

ARGAN

Well, he is the nephew of Mr. Purgon, and the son of his brother-in-law, Mr. Diafoirus; and this son is called Thomas Diafoirus, and not Cléante. Mr. Fleurant and I decided upon this match this morning, and to-morrow this future son-in-law will be brought to me by his father.... What is the matter, you look all scared?

ANGÉLIQUE

It is because, father, I see that you have been speaking of one person, and I of another.

TOINETTE

What! Sir, you have formed such a queer project as that, and, with all the wealth you possess, you want to marry your daughter to a doctor?

ARGAN

What business is it of yours, you impudent jade?

TOINETTE

Gently, gently. You always begin by abuse. Can we not reason together without getting into a rage? Come, let us speak quietly. What reason have you, if you please, for such a marriage?

ARGAN

My reason is, that seeing myself infirm and sick, I wish to have a son-in-law and relatives who are doctors, in order to secure their kind assistance in my illness, to have in my family the fountain-head of those remedies which are necessary to me, and to be within reach of consultations and prescriptions.

TOINETTE

Very well; at least that is giving a reason, and there is a certain pleasure in answering one another calmly. But now, Sir, on your conscience, do you really and truly believe that you are ill?

ARGAN

Believe that I am ill, you jade? Believe that I am ill, you impudent hussy?

TOINETTE

Very well, then, Sir, you are ill; don't let us quarrel about that. Yes, you are very ill, I agree with you upon that point, more ill even than you think. Now, is that settled? But your daughter is to marry a husband for herself, and as she is not ill, what is the use of giving her a doctor?

ARGAN

It is for my sake that I give her this doctor, and a good daughter ought to be delighted to marry for the sake of her father's health.

TOINETTE

In good troth, Sir, shall I, as a friend, give you a piece of advice?

ARGAN

What is this advice?

TOINETTE

Not to think of this match.

ARGAN

And your reason?

TOINETTE

The reason is that your daughter will never consent to it.

ARGAN

My daughter will not consent to it?

TOINETTE

No.

ARGAN

My daughter?

TOINETTE

Your daughter. She will tell you that she has no need of Mr. Diafoirus, nor of his son, Mr. Thomas Diafoirus, nor all the Diafoiruses in the world.

ARGAN

But I have need of them. Besides, the match is more advantageous than you think. Mr. Diafoirus has only this son for his heir; and, moreover, Mr. Purgon, who has neither wife nor child, gives all he has in favour of this marriage; and Mr. Purgon is man worth eight thousand francs a year.

TOINETTE

What a lot of people he must have killed to have become so rich!

ARGAN

Eight thousand francs is something, without counting the property of the father.

TOINETTE

That is very well, Sir, but, all the same, I advise you, between ourselves, to choose another husband for her; she is not of a make to become a Mrs. Diafoirus.

ARGAN

But I will have it so.

TOINETTE

Fie! nonsense! Don't speak like that.

ARGAN

Don't speak like that? Why not?

TOINETTE

Dear me, no, don't.

ARGAN

And why should I not speak like that?

TOINETTE

People will say that you don't know what you are talking about.

ARGAN

People will say all they like, but I tell you that I will have her make my promise good.

TOINETTE

I feel sure that she won't.

ARGAN

Then I will force her to do it.

TOINETTE

She will not do it, I tell you.

ARGAN

She will, or I will shut her up in a convent.

TOINETTE

You?

ARGAN

I.

TOINETTE

Good!

ARGAN

How good?

TOINETTE

You will not shut her up in a convent.

ARGAN

I shall not shut her up in a convent?

TOINETTE

No.

ARGAN

No?

TOINETTE

No.

ARGAN

Well, this is cool! I shall not put my daughter in a convent if I like!

TOINETTE

No, I tell you.

ARGAN

And who will hinder me?

TOINETTE

You yourself.

ARGAN

Myself?

TOINETTE

You will never have the heart to do it.

ARGAN
I shall.

TOINETTE
You are joking.

ARGAN
I am not joking.

TOINETTE
Fatherly love will hinder you.

ARGAN
It will not hinder me.

TOINETTE
A little tear or two, her arms thrown round your neck, Or "My darling little papa," said very tenderly, will be enough to touch your heart.

ARGAN
All that will be useless.

TOINETTE
Oh yes!

ARGAN
I tell you that nothing will move me.

TOINETTE
Rubbish!

ARGAN
You have no business to say "Rubbish."

TOINETTE
I know you well enough; you are naturally kind-hearted.

ARGAN [Angrily]
I am not kind-hearted, and I am ill-natured when I like.

TOINETTE
Gently, Sir, you forget that you are ill.

ARGAN
I command her to prepare herself to take the husband I have fixed upon.

TOINETTE

And I decidedly forbid her to do anything of the kind.

ARGAN
What have we come to? And what boldness is this for a scrub of a servant to speak in such a way before her master?

TOINETTE
When a master does not consider what he is doing, a sensible servant should set him right.

ARGAN [Running after **TOINETTE**]
Ah, impudent girl, I will kill you!

TOINETTE [Avoiding **ARGAN**, and putting the chair between her and him]
It is my duty to oppose what would be a dishonour to you.

ARGAN [Running after **TOINETTE** with his cane in his hand]
Come here, come here, let me teach you how to speak.

TOINETTE [Running to the opposite side of the chair]
I interest myself in your affairs as I ought to do, and I don't wish to see you commit any folly.

ARGAN [As before]
Jade!

TOINETTE [As before]
No, I will never consent to this marriage.

ARGAN [As before]
Worthless hussy!

TOINETTE [As before]
I won't have her marry your Thomas Diafoirus.

ARGAN [As before]
Vixen!

TOINETTE [As before]
She will obey me sooner than you.

ARGAN [Stopping]
Angélique, won't you stop that jade for me?

ANGÉLIQUE
Ah! father, don't make yourself ill.

ARGAN [To **ANGÉLIQUE**]
If you don't stop her, I will refuse you my blessing.

TOINETTE [Going away]
And I will disinherit her if she obeys you.

ARGAN [Throwing himself into his chair]
Ah! I am done for. It is enough to kill me!

SCENE VI

BÉLINE, ARGAN.

ARGAN
Ah! come near, my wife.

BÉLINE
What ails you, my poor, dear husband?

ARGAN
Come to my help.

BÉLINE
What is the matter, my little darling child?

ARGAN
My love.

BÉLINE
My love.

ARGAN
They have just put me in a rage.

BÉLINE
Alas! my poor little husband! How was that, my own dear pet?

ARGAN
That jade of yours, Toinette, has grown more insolent than ever.

BÉLINE
Don't excite yourself.

ARGAN
She has put me in a rage, my dove.

BÉLINE
Gently, my child.

ARGAN

She has been thwarting me for the last hour about everything I want to do.

BÉLINE

There, there; never mind.

ARGAN

And has had the impudence to say that I am not ill.

BÉLINE

She is an impertinent hussy.

ARGAN

You know, my soul, what the truth is?

BÉLINE

Yes, my darling, she is wrong.

ARGAN

My own dear, that jade will be the death of me.

BÉLINE

Now, don't, don't.

ARGAN

She is the cause of all my bile.

BÉLINE

Don't be so angry.

ARGAN

And I have asked you ever so many times to send her away.

BÉLINE

Alas! my child, there is no servant without defects. We are obliged to put up at times with their bad qualities on account of their good ones. The girl is skilful, careful, diligent, and, above all, honest; and you know that in our days we must be very careful what people we take into our house. I say, Toinette.

SCENE VII

ARGAN, BÉLINE, TOINETTE.

TOINETTE
Madam.

BÉLINE

How is this? Why do you put my husband in a passion?

TOINETTE [In a soft tone]
I, Madam? Alas! I don't know what you mean, and my only aim is to please master in everything.

ARGAN
Ah! the deceitful girl!

TOINETTE
He said to us that he wished to marry his daughter to the son of Mr. Diafoirus. I told him that I thought the match very advantageous for her, but that I believed he would do better to put her in a convent.

BÉLINE
There is not much harm in that, and I think that she is right.

ARGAN
Ah! deary, do you believe her? She is a vile girl, and has said a hundred insolent things to me.

BÉLINE
Well, I believe you, my dear. Come, compose yourself; and you, Toinette, listen to me. If ever you make my husband angry again, I will send you away. Come, give me his fur cloak and some pillows, that I may make him comfortable in his arm-chair. You are all anyhow. Pull your night-cap right down over your ears; there is nothing that gives people such bad colds as letting in the air through the ears.

ARGAN
Ah, deary! how much obliged I am to you for all the care you take of me.

BÉLINE [Adjusting the pillows, which she puts round him]
Raise yourself a little for me to put this under you. Let us put this one for you to lean upon, and this one on the other side; this one behind your back, and this other to support your head.

TOINETTE [Clapping a pillow rudely on his head]
And this other to keep you from the evening damp.

ARGAN [Rising angrily, and throwing the pillows after **TOINETTE**, who runs away]
Ah, wretch! you want to smother me.

SCENE VIII

ARGAN, BÉLINE.

BÉLINE
Now, now; what is it again?

ARGAN [Throwing himself in his chair]
Ah! I can hold out no longer.

BÉLINE

But why do you fly into such a passion? she thought she was doing right.

ARGAN

You don't know, darling, the wickedness of that villainous baggage. She has altogether upset me, and I shall want more than eight different mixtures and twelve injections to remedy the evil.

BÉLINE

Come, come, my dearie, compose yourself a little.

ARGAN

Lovey, you are my only consolation.

BÉLINE

Poor little pet!

ARGAN

To repay you for all the love you have for me, my darling, I will, as I told you, make my will.

BÉLINE

Ah, my soul! do not let us speak of that, I beseech you. I cannot bear to think of it, and the very word "will" makes me die of grief.

ARGAN

I had asked you to speak to our notary about it.

BÉLINE

There he is, close at hand; I have brought him with me.

ARGAN

Make him come in then, my life!

BÉLINE

Alas! my darling, when a woman loves her husband so much, she finds it almost impossible to think of these things.

SCENE IX

MR. DE BONNEFOI, BÉLINE, ARGAN.

ARGAN

Come here, Mr. de Bonnefoi, come here. Take a seat, if you please. My wife tells me, Sir, that you are a very honest man, and altogether one of her friends; I have therefore asked her to speak to you about a will which I wish to make.

BÉLINE

Alas! I cannot speak of those things.

MR. DE BONNEFOI

She has fully explained to me your intentions, Sir, and what you mean to do for her. But I have to tell you that you can give nothing to your wife by will.

ARGAN

But why so?

MR. DE BONNEFOI

It is against custom. If you were in a district where statute law prevailed, the thing could be done; but in Paris, and in almost all places governed by custom, it cannot be done; and the will would be held void. The only settlement that man and wife can make on each other is by mutual donation while they are alive, and even then there must be no children from either that marriage or from any previous marriage at the decease of the first who dies.

ARGAN

It's a very impertinent custom that a husband can leave nothing to a wife whom he loves, by whom he is tenderly loved, and who takes so much care of him. I should like to consult my own advocate to see what I can do.

MR. DE BONNEFOI

It is not to an advocate that you must apply; for they are very particular on this point and think it a great crime to bestow one's property contrary to the law. They are people to make difficulties, and are ignorant of the bylaws of conscience. There are others whom you may consult with advantage on that point, and who have expedients for gently overriding the law, and for rendering just that which is not allowed. These know how to smooth over the difficulties of an affair, and to find the means of eluding custom by some indirect advantage. Without that, what would become of us every day? We must make things easy; otherwise we should do nothing, and I wouldn't give a penny for our business.

ARGAN

My wife had rightly told me, Sir, that you were a very clever and honest man. What can I do, pray, to give her my fortune and deprive my children of it?

MR. DE BONNEFOI

What you can do? You can discreetly choose a friend of your wife, to whom you will give all you own in due form by your will, and that friend will give it up to her afterwards; or else you can sign a great many safe bonds in favour of various creditors who will lend their names to your wife, and in whose hands they will leave a declaration that what was done was only to serve her. You can also in your lifetime put in her hands ready money and bills which you can make payable to bearer.

BÉLINE

Alas! you must not trouble yourself about all that. If I lose you, my child, I will stay no longer in the world.

ARGAN

My darling!

BÉLINE
Yes, my pet, if I were unfortunate enough to lose you ...

ARGAN
My dear wifey!

BÉLINE
Life would be nothing to me.

ARGAN
My love!

BÉLINE
And I would follow you to the grave, to show you all the tenderness I feel for you.

ARGAN
You will break my heart, deary; comfort yourself, I beseech you.

MR. DE BONNEFOI [To **BÉLINE**]
These tears are unseasonable; things have not come to that yet.

BÉLINE
Ah, Sir! you don't know what it is to have a husband one loves tenderly.

ARGAN
All the regret I shall have, if I die, my darling, will be to have no child from you. Mr. Purgon told me he would make me have one.

MR. DE BONNEFOI
That may come still.

ARGAN
I must make my will, deary, according to what this gentleman advises; but, out of precaution, I will give you the twenty thousand francs in gold which I have in the wainscoting of the recess of my room, and two bills payable to bearer which are due to me, one from Mr. Damon, the other from Mr. Géronte.

BÉLINE
No, no! I will have nothing to do with all that. Ah! How much do you say there is in the recess?

ARGAN
Twenty thousand francs, darling.

BÉLINE
Don't speak to me of your money, I beseech you. Ah! How much are the two bills for?

ARGAN
One, my love, is for four thousand francs, and the other for six thousand.

BÉLINE
All the wealth in the world, my soul, is nothing to me compared to you.

MR. DE BONNEFOI [To **ARGAN**]
Shall we draw up the will?

ARGAN
Yes, Sir. But we shall be more comfortable in my own little study. Help me, my love.

BÉLINE
Come, my poor, dear child.

SCENE X

ANGÉLIQUE, TOINETTE.

TOINETTE
They are shut up with the notary, and I heard something about a will; your mother-in-law doesn't go to sleep; it is, no doubt, some conspiracy of hers against your interests to which she is urging your father.

ANGÉLIQUE
Let him dispose of his money as he likes, as long as he does not dispose of my heart in the same way. You see, Toinette, to what violence it is subjected. Do not forsake me, I beseech you, in this my extremity.

TOINETTE
I forsake you! I had rather die. In vain does your stepmother try to take me into her confidence, and make me espouse her interests. I never could like her, and I have always been on your side. Trust me, I will do every thing to serve you. But, in order to serve you more effectually, I shall change my tactics, hide my wish to help you, and affect to enter into the feelings of your father and your stepmother.

ANGÉLIQUE
Try, I beseech you, to let Cléante know about the marriage they have decided upon.

TOINETTE
I have nobody to employ for that duty but the old usurer Punchinello, my lover; it will cost me a few honeyed words, which I am most willing to spend for you. To-day it is too late for that, but to-morrow morning early I will send for him, and he will be delighted to ...

SCENE XI

BÉLINE in the house, **ANGÉLIQUE, TOINETTE.**

BÉLINE
Toinette.

TOINETTE [To **ANGÉLIQUE**]
I am called away. Good night. Trust me.

FIRST INTERLUDE

ACT II

SCENE I

CLÉANTE, TOINETTE

TOINETTE [Not recognising **CLÉANTE**]
What is it you want, Sir?

CLÉANTE
What do I want?

TOINETTE
Ah! ah! is it you? What a surprise! What are you coming here for?

CLÉANTE
To learn my destiny, to speak to the lovely Angélique, to consult the feelings of her heart, and to ask her what she means to do about this fatal marriage of which I have been told.

TOINETTE
Very well; but no one speaks so easily as all that to Angélique; you must take precautions, and you have been told how narrowly she is watched. She never goes out, nor does she see anybody. It was through the curiosity of an old aunt that we obtained leave to go to the play where your love began, and we have taken good care not to say anything about it.

CLÉANTE
Therefore am I not here as Cléante, nor as her lover, but as the friend of her music-master, from whom I have obtained leave to say that I have come in his stead.

TOINETTE
Here is her father; withdraw a little and let me tell him who you are.

SCENE II

ARGAN, TOINETTE.

ARGAN [Thinking himself alone]

Mr. Purgon told me that I was to walk twelve times to and fro in my room every morning, but I forgot to ask him whether it should be lengthways or across.

TOINETTE

Sir, here is a gentleman ...

ARGAN

Speak in a lower tone, you jade; you split my head open; and you forget that we should never speak so loud to sick people.

TOINETTE

I wanted to tell you, Sir ...

ARGAN

Speak low, I tell you.

TOINETTE

Sir ...

[She moves her lips as if she were speaking.

ARGAN

What?

TOINETTE

I tell you that ... [As before]

ARGAN

What is it you say?

TOINETTE [Aloud]

I say that there is a gentleman here who wants to speak to you.

ARGAN

Let him come in.

SCENE III

ARGAN, CLÉANTE, TOINETTE.

CLÉANTE

Sir.

TOINETTE [To **CLÉANTE**]

Do not speak so loud, for fear of splitting open the head of Mr. Argan.

CLÉANTE
Sir, I am delighted to find you up, and to see you better.

TOINETTE [Affecting to be angry]
How! better? It is false; master is always ill.

CLÉANTE
I had heard that your master was better, and I think that he looks well in the face.

TOINETTE
What do you mean by his looking well in the face? He looks very bad, and it is only impertinent folks who say that he is better; he never was so ill in his life.

ARGAN
She is right.

TOINETTE
He walks, sleeps, eats, and drinks, like other folks, but that does not hinder him from being very ill.

ARGAN
Quite true.

CLÉANTE
I am heartily sorry for it, Sir. I am sent by your daughter's music-master; he was obliged to go into the country for a few days, and as I am his intimate friend, he has asked me to come here in his place, to go on with the lessons, for fear that, if they were discontinued, she should forget what she has already learnt.

ARGAN
Very well.
[To **TOINETTE**]
Call Angélique.

TOINETTE
I think, Sir, It would be better to take the gentleman to her room.

ARGAN
No, make her come here.

TOINETTE
He cannot give her a good lesson if they are not left alone.

ARGAN
Oh! yes, he can.

TOINETTE

Sir, it will stun you; and you should have nothing to disturb you in the state of health you are in.

ARGAN
No, no; I like music, and I should be glad to ... Ah! here she is.
[To **TOINETTE**]
Go and see if my wife is dressed.

SCENE IV

ARGAN, ANGÉLIQUE, CLÉANTE.

ARGAN
Come, my daughter, your music-master is gone into the country, and here is a person whom he sends instead, to give you your lesson.

ANGÉLIQUE [Recognising **CLÉANTE**]
O heavens!

ARGAN
What is the matter? Why this surprise?

ANGÉLIQUE
It is ...

ARGAN
What can disturb you in that manner?

ANGÉLIQUE
It is such a strange coincidence.

ARGAN
How so?

ANGÉLIQUE
I dreamt last night that I was in the greatest trouble imaginable, and that some one exactly like this gentleman came to me. I asked him to help me, and presently he saved me from the great trouble I was in. My surprise was very great to meet unexpectedly, on my coming here, him of whom I had been dreaming all night.

CLÉANTE
It is no small happiness to occupy your thoughts whether sleeping or waking, and my delight would be great indeed if you were in any trouble out of which you would think me worthy of delivering you. There is nothing that I would not do for ...

ARGAN, ANGÉLIQUE, CLÉANTE, TOINETTE.

TOINETTE [To **ARGAN**]
Indeed, Sir, I am of your opinion now, and I unsay all that I said yesterday. Here are Mr. Diafoirus the father, and Mr. Diafoirus the son, who are coming to visit you. How well provided with a son-in-law you will be! You will see the best-made young fellow in the world, and the most intellectual. He said but two words to me, it is true, but I was struck with them, and your daughter will be delighted with him.

ARGAN [To **CLÉANTE**, who moves as if to go]
Do not go, Sir. I am about, as you see, to marry my daughter, and they have just brought her future husband, whom she has not as yet seen.

CLÉANTE
You do me great honour, Sir, in wishing me to be witness of such a pleasant interview.

ARGAN
He is the son of a clever doctor, and the marriage will take place in four days.

CLÉANTE
Indeed!

ARGAN
Please inform her music-master of it, that he may be at the wedding.

CLÉANTE
I will not fail to do so.

ARGAN
And I invite you also.

CLÉANTE
You do me too much honour.

TOINETTE
Come, make room; here they are.

SCENE VI

MR. DIAFOIRUS, THOMAS DIAFOIRUS, ARGAN, ANGÉLIQUE, CLÉANTE, TOINETTE, SERVANTS.

ARGAN [Putting up his hand to his night-cap without taking it off]
Mr. Purgon has forbidden me to uncover my head. You belong to the profession, and know what would be the consequence if I did so.

MR. DIAFOIRUS
We are bound in all our visits to bring relief to invalids, and not to injure them.

[**MR. ARGAN** and **MR. DIAFOIRUS** speak at the same time.

ARGAN
I receive, Sir ...

MR. DIAFOIRUS
We come here, Sir ...

ARGAN
With great joy ...

MR. DIAFOIRUS
My son Thomas and myself ...

ARGAN
The honour you do me ...

MR. DIAFOIRUS
To declare to you, Sir ...

ARGAN
And I wish ...

MR. DIAFOIRUS
The delight we are in ...

ARGAN
I could have gone to your house ...

MR. DIAFOIRUS
At the favour you do us ...

ARGAN
To assure you of it ...

MR. DIAFOIRUS
In so kindly admitting us ...

ARGAN
But you know, Sir ...

MR. DIAFOIRUS
To the honour, Sir ...

ARGAN

What it is to be a poor invalid ...

MR. DIAFOIRUS
Of your alliance ...

ARGAN
Who can only ...

MR. DIAFOIRUS
And assure you ...

ARGAN
Tell you here....

MR. DIAFOIRUS
That in all that depends on our knowledge....

ARGAN
That he will seize every opportunity....

MR. DIAFOIRUS
As well as in any other way....

ARGAN
To show you, Sir....

MR. DIAFOIRUS
That we shall ever be ready, Sir....

ARGAN
That he is entirely at your service....

MR. DIAFOIRUS
To show you our zeal.
[To his **SON**]
Now, Thomas, come forward, and pay your respects.

THOMAS DIAFOIRUS [To **MR. DIAFOIRUS**]
Ought I not to begin with the father?

MR. DIAFOIRUS
Yes.

THOMAS DIAFOIRUS [To **ARGAN**]
Sir, I come to salute, acknowledge, cherish, and revere in you a second father; but a second father to whom I owe more, I make bold to say, than to the first. The first gave me birth; but you have chosen me. He received me by necessity, but you have accepted me by choice. What I have from him is of the body, corporal; what I hold from you is of the will, voluntary; and in so much the more as the mental faculties

are above the corporal, in so much the more do I hold precious this future affiliation, for which I come beforehand to-day to render you my most humble and most respectful homage.

TOINETTE
Long life to the colleges which send such clever people into the world!

THOMAS DIAFOIRUS [To **MR. DIAFOIRUS**]
Has this been said to your satisfaction, father?

MR. DIAFOIRUS
Optime.

ARGAN [To **ANGÉLIQUE**]
Come, bow to this gentleman.

THOMAS DIAFOIRUS [To **MR. DIAFOIRUS**]
Shall I kiss?

MR. DIAFOIRUS
Yes, yes.

THOMAS DIAFOIRUS [To **ANGÉLIQUE**]
Madam, it is with justice that heaven has given you the name of stepmother, since we see in you steps towards the perfect beauty which....[2]

ARGAN [To **THOMAS DIAFOIRUS**]
It is not to my wife, but to my daughter, that you are speaking.

THOMAS DIAFOIRUS
Where is she?

ARGAN
She will soon come.

THOMAS DIAFOIRUS
Shall I wait, father, till she comes?

MR. DIAFOIRUS
No; go through your compliments to the young lady in the meantime.

THOMAS DIAFOIRUS
Madam, as the statue of Memnon gave forth a harmonious sound when it was struck by the first rays of the sun, in like manner do I experience a sweet rapture at the apparition of this sun of your beauty. As the naturalists remark that the flower styled heliotrope always turns towards the star of day, so will my heart for ever turn towards the resplendent stars of your adorable eyes as to its only pole. Suffer me, then, Madam, to make to-day on the altar of your charms the offering of a heart which longs for and is ambitious of no greater glory than to be till death, Madam, your most humble, most obedient, most faithful servant and husband.

TOINETTE

Ah! See what it is to study, and how one learns to say fine things!

ARGAN [To **CLÉANTE**]

Well! what do you say to that?

CLÉANTE

The gentleman does wonders, and if he is as good a doctor as he is an orator, it will be most pleasant to be one of his patients.

TOINETTE

Certainly, it will be something admirable if his cures are as wonderful as his speeches.

ARGAN

Now, quick, my chair; and seats for everybody.

[**SERVANTS** bring chairs.

Sit down here, my daughter.
[To **MR. DIAFOIRUS**]
You see, Sir, that everybody admires your son; and I think you very fortunate in being the father of such a fine young man.

MR. DIAFOIRUS

Sir, it is not because I am his father, but I can boast that I have reason to be satisfied with him, and that all those who see him speak of him as of a youth without guile. He has not a very lively imagination, nor that sparkling wit which is found in some others; but it is this which has always made me augur well of his judgment, a quality required for the exercise of our art. As a child he never was what is called sharp or lively. He was always gentle, peaceful, taciturn, never saying a word, and never playing at any of those little pastimes that we call children's games. It was found most difficult to teach him to read, and he was nine years old before he knew his letters. A good omen, I used to say to myself; trees slow of growth bear the best fruit. We engrave on marble with much more difficulty than on sand, but the result is more lasting; and that dulness of apprehension, that heaviness of imagination, is a mark of a sound judgment in the future. When I sent him to college, he found it hard work, but he stuck to his duty, and bore up with obstinacy against all difficulties. His tutors always praised him for his assiduity and the trouble he took. In short, by dint of continual hammering, he at last succeeded gloriously in obtaining his degree; and I can say, without vanity, that from that time till now there has been no candidate who has made more noise than he in all the disputations of our school. There he has rendered himself formidable, and no debate passes but he goes and argues loudly and to the last extreme on the opposite side. He is firm in dispute, strong as a Turk in his principles, never changes his opinion, and pursues an argument to the last recesses of logic. But, above all things, what pleases me in him, and what I am glad to see him follow my example in, is that he is blindly attached to the opinions of the ancients, and that he would never understand nor listen to the reasons and the experiences of the pretended discoveries of our century concerning the circulation of the blood and other opinions of the same stamp.[3]

THOMAS DIAFOIRUS [Pulling out of his pocket a long paper rolled up, and presenting it to **ANGÉLIQUE**]

I have upheld against these circulators a thesis which, with the permission

[Bowing to **ARGAN**.

—of this gentleman, I venture to present to the young lady as the first-fruits of my genius.

ANGÉLIQUE
Sir, it is a useless piece of furniture to me; I do not understand these things.

TOINETTE [Taking the paper]
Never mind; give it all the same; the picture will be of use, and we will adorn our attic with it.

THOMAS DIAFOIRUS [Again bowing to **ANGÉLIQUE**]
With the permission of this gentleman, I invite you to come one of these days to amuse yourself by assisting at the dissection of a woman upon whose body I am to give lectures.

TOINETTE
The treat will be most welcome. There are some who give the pleasure of seeing a play to their lady-love; but a dissection is much more gallant.

MR. DIAFOIRUS
Moreover, in respect to the qualities required for marriage, I assure you that he is all you could wish, and that his children will be strong and healthy.

ARGAN
Do you not intend, Sir, to push his way at court, and obtain for him the post of physician there?

MR. DIAFOIRUS
To tell you the truth, I have never had any predilection to practice with the great; it never seemed pleasant to me, and I have found that it is better for us to confine ourselves to the ordinary public. Ordinary people are more convenient; you are accountable to nobody for your actions, and as long as you follow the common rules laid down by the faculty, there is no necessity to trouble yourself about the result. What is vexatious among people of rank is that, when they are ill, they positively expect their doctor to cure them.

TOINETTE
How very absurd! How impertinent of them to ask of you doctors to cure them! You are not placed near them for that, but only to receive your fees and to prescribe remedies. It is their own look-out to get well if they can.

MR. DIAFOIRUS
Quite so. We are only bound to treat people according to form.

ARGAN [To **CLÉANTE**]
Sir, please make my daughter sing before the company.

CLÉANTE
I was waiting for your commands, Sir; and I propose, in order to amuse the company, to sing with the young lady an operetta which has lately come out.

[To **ANGÉLIQUE**, giving her a paper.

There is your part.

ANGÉLIQUE
Mine?

CLÉANTE [Aside to **ANGÉLIQUE**]
Don't refuse, pray; but let me explain to you what is the scene we must sing.
[Aloud]
I have no voice; but in this case it is sufficient if I make myself understood; and you must have the
goodness to excuse me, because I am under the necessity of making the young lady sing.

ARGAN
Are the verses pretty?

CLÉANTE
It is really nothing but a small extempore opera, and what you will hear is only rhythmical prose or a
kind of irregular verse, such as passion and necessity make two people utter.

ARGAN
Very well; let us hear.

CLÉANTE
The subject of the scene is as follows. A shepherd was paying every attention to the beauties of a play,
when he was disturbed by a noise close to him, and on turning round he saw a scoundrel who, with
insolent language, was annoying a young shepherdess. He immediately espoused the cause of a sex to
which all men owe homage; and after having chastised the brute for his insolence, he came near the
shepherdess to comfort her. He sees a young girl with the most beautiful eyes he has ever beheld, who
is shedding tears which he thinks the most precious in the world. Alas! says he to himself, can any one
be capable of insulting such charms? Where is the unfeeling wretch, the barbarous man to be found
who will not feel touched by such tears? He endeavours to stop those beautiful tears, and the lovely
shepherdess takes the opportunity of thanking him for the slight service he has rendered her. But she
does it in a manner so touching, so tender, and so passionate that the shepherd cannot resist it, and
each word, each look is a burning shaft which penetrates his heart. Is there anything in the world worthy
of such thanks? and what will not one do, what service and what danger will not one be delighted to run
to attract upon oneself even for a moment the touching sweetness of so grateful a heart? The whole
play was acted without his paying any more attention to it; yet he complains that it was too short, since
the end separates him from his lovely shepherdess. From that moment, from that first sight, he carries
away with him a love which has the strength of a passion of many years. He now feels all the pangs of
absence, and is tormented in no longer seeing what he beheld for so short a time. He tries every means
to meet again with a sight so dear to him, and the remembrance of which pursues him day and night.
But the great watch which is kept over his shepherdess deprives him of all the power of doing so. The
violence of his passion urges him to ask in marriage the adorable beauty without whom he can no longer
live, and he obtains from her the permission of doing so, by means of a note that he has succeeded in
sending to her. But he is told in the meantime that the father of her whom he loves has decided upon
marrying her to another, and that everything is being got ready to celebrate the wedding. Judge what a

cruel wound for the heart of that poor shepherd! Behold him suffering from this mortal blow; he cannot bear the dreadful idea of seeing her he loves in the arms of another; and in his despair he finds the means of introducing himself into the house of his shepherdess, in order to learn her feelings and to hear from her the fate he must expect. There he sees everything ready for what he fears; he sees the unworthy rival whom the caprice of a father opposes to the tenderness of his love; he sees that ridiculous rival triumphant near the lovely shepherdess, as if already assured of his conquest. Such a sight fills him with a wrath he can hardly master. He looks despairingly at her whom he adores, but the respect he has for her and the presence of her father prevent him from speaking except with his eyes. At last he breaks through all restraint, and the greatness of his love forces him to speak as follows.

[He sings.

Phyllis, too sharp a pain you bid me bear;
Break this stern silence, tell me what to fear;
Disclose your thoughts, and bid them open lie
To tell me if I live or die.

ANGÉLIQUE
The marriage preparations sadden me.
O'erwhelmed with sorrow,
My eyes I lift to heaven; I strive to pray,
Then gaze on you and sigh. No more I say.

CLÉANTE
Tircis, who fain would woo,
Tell him, Phyllis, is it true,
Is he so blest by your sweet grace
As in your heart to find a place?

ANGÉLIQUE
I may not hide it, in this dire extreme,
Tircis, I own for you my love....

CLÉANTE
O blessed words! am I indeed so blest?
Repeat them, Phyllis; set my doubts at rest.

ANGÉLIQUE
I love you, Tircis!

CLÉANTE
Ah! Phyllis, once again.

ANGÉLIQUE
I love you, Tircis!

CLÉANTE
Alas! I fain

A hundred times would hearken to that strain.

ANGÉLIQUE
I love you! I love you!
Tircis, I love you!

CLÉANTE
Ye kings and gods who, from your eternal seat,
Behold the world of men beneath your feet,
Can you possess a happiness more sweet?
My Phyllis! one dark haunting fear
Our peaceful joy disturbs unsought;
A rival may my homage share.

ANGÉLIQUE
Ah! worse than death is such a thought!
Its presence equal torment is
To both, and mars my bliss.

CLÉANTE
Your father to his vow would subject you.

ANGÉLIQUE
Ah! welcome death before I prove untrue.

ARGAN
And what does the father say to all that?

CLÉANTE
Nothing.

ARGAN
Then that father is a fool to put up with those silly things, without saying a word!

CLÉANTE [Trying to go on singing]
Ah! my love....

ARGAN
No; no; that will do. An opera like that is in very bad taste. The shepherd Tircis is an impertinent fellow, and the shepherdess Phyllis an impudent girl to speak in that way in the presence of her father.
[To **ANGÉLIQUE**]
Show me that paper. Ah! ah! and where are the words that you have just sung? This is only the music.

CLÉANTE
Are you not aware, Sir, that the way of writing the words with the notes themselves has been lately discovered?

ARGAN

Has it? Good-bye for the present. We could have done very well without your impertinent opera.

CLÉANTE
I thought I should amuse you.

ARGAN
Foolish things do not amuse, Sir. Ah! here is my wife.

SCENE VII

BÉLINE, ARGAN, ANGÉLIQUE, MR. DIAFOIRUS, T. DIAFOIRUS, TOINETTE.

ARGAN
My love, here is the son of Mr. Diafoirus.

THOMAS DIAFOIRUS
Madam, it is with justice that heaven has given you the title of stepmother, since we see in you steps....

BÉLINE
Sir, I am delighted to have come here just in time to see you.

THOMAS DIAFOIRUS
Since we see in you ... since we see in you.... Madam, you have interrupted me in the middle of my period, and have troubled my memory.

MR. DIAFOIRUS
Keep it for another time.

ARGAN
I wish, my dear, that you had been here just now.

TOINETTE
Ah! Madam, how much you have lost by not being at the second father, the statue of Memnon, and the flower styled heliotrope.

ARGAN
Come, my daughter, shake hands with this gentleman, and pledge him your troth.

ANGÉLIQUE
Father!

ARGAN
Well? What do you mean by "Father"?

ANGÉLIQUE

I beseech you not to be in such a hurry; give us time to become acquainted with each other, and to see grow in us that sympathy so necessary to a perfect union.

THOMAS DIAFOIRUS
As far as I am concerned, Madam, it is already full-grown within me, and there is no occasion for me to wait.

ANGÉLIQUE
I am not so quick as you are, Sir, and I must confess that your merit has not yet made enough impression on my heart.

ARGAN
Oh! nonsense! There will be time enough for the impression to be made after you are married.

ANGÉLIQUE
Ah! my father, give me time, I beseech you! Marriage is a chain which should never be imposed by force. And if this gentleman is a man of honour, he ought not to accept a person who would be his only by force.

THOMAS DIAFOIRUS
Nego consequentiam. I can be a man of honour, Madam, and at the same time accept you from the hands of your father.

ANGÉLIQUE
To do violence to any one is a strange way of setting about inspiring love.

THOMAS DIAFOIRUS
We read in the ancients, Madam, that it was their custom to carry off by main force from their father's house the maiden they wished to marry, so that the latter might not seem to fly of her own accord into the arms of a man.

ANGÉLIQUE
The ancients, Sir, are the ancients; but we are the moderns. Pretences are not necessary in our age; and when a marriage pleases us, we know very well how to go to it without being dragged by force. Have a little patience; if you love me, Sir, you ought to do what I wish.

THOMAS DIAFOIRUS
Certainly, Madam, but without prejudice to the interest of my love.

ANGÉLIQUE
But the greatest mark of love is to submit to the will of her who is loved.

THOMAS DIAFOIRUS
Distinguo, Madam. In what does not regard the possession of her, concedo; but in what regards it, nego.

TOINETTE [To **ANGÉLIQUE**]
It is in vain for you to argue. This gentleman is bran new from college, and will be more than a match for you. Why resist, and refuse the glory of belonging to the faculty?

BÉLINE

She may have some other inclination in her head.

ANGÉLIQUE

If I had, Madam, it would be such as reason and honour allow.

ARGAN

Heyday! I am acting a pleasant part here!

BÉLINE

If I were you, my child, I would not force her to marry; I know very well what I should do.

ANGÉLIQUE

I know what you mean, Madam, and how kind you are to me; but it may be hoped that your advice may not be fortunate enough to be followed.

BÉLINE

That is because well-brought-up and good children, like you, scorn to be obedient to the will of their fathers. Obedience was all very well in former times.

ANGÉLIQUE

The duty of a daughter has its limits, Madam, and neither reason nor law extend it to all things.

BÉLINE

Which means that your thoughts are all in favor of marriage, but that you will choose a husband for yourself.

ANGÉLIQUE

If my father will not give me a husband I like, at least I beseech him not to force me to marry one I can never love.

ARGAN

Gentlemen, I beg your pardon for all this.

ANGÉLIQUE

We all have our own end in marrying. For my part, as I only want a husband that I can love sincerely, and as I intend to consecrate my whole life to him, I feel bound, I confess, to be cautious. There are some who marry simply to free themselves from the yoke of their parents, and to be at liberty to do all they like. There are others, Madam, who see in marriage only a matter of mere interest; who marry only to get a settlement, and to enrich themselves by the death of those they marry. They pass without scruple from husband to husband, with an eye to their possessions. These, no doubt, Madam, are not so difficult to satisfy, and care little what the husband is like.

BÉLINE

You are very full of reasoning to-day. I wonder what you mean by this.

ANGÉLIQUE

I, Madam? What can I mean but what I say?

BÉLINE
You are such a simpleton, my dear, that one can hardly bear with you.

ANGÉLIQUE
You would like to extract from me some rude answer; but I warn you that you will not have the pleasure of doing so.

BÉLINE
Nothing can equal your impertinence.

ANGÉLIQUE
It is of no use, Madam; you will not.

BÉLINE
And you have a ridiculous pride, an impertinent presumption, which makes you the scorn of everybody.

ANGÉLIQUE
All this will be useless, Madam. I shall be quiet in spite of you; and to take away from you all hope of succeeding in what you wish, I will withdraw from your presence.

SCENE VIII

ARGAN, BÉLINE, MR. DIAFOIRUS, T. DIAFOIRUS, TOINETTE.

ARGAN [To **ANGÉLIQUE**, as she goes away]
Listen to me! Of two things, one. Either you will marry this gentleman or you will go into a convent. I give you four days to consider.
[To **BÉLINE**]
Don't be anxious; I will bring her to reason.

BÉLINE
I am sorry to leave you, my child; but I have some important business which calls me to town. I shall soon be back.

ARGAN
Go, my darling; call upon the notary, and tell him to be quick about you know what.

BÉLINE
Good-bye, my child.

ARGAN
Good-bye, deary.

SCENE IX

ARGAN, MR. DIAFOIRUS, T. DIAFOIRUS, TOINETTE.

ARGAN
How much this woman loves me; it is perfectly incredible.

MR. DIAFOIRUS
We shall now take our leave of you, Sir.

ARGAN
I beg of you, Sir, to tell me how I am.

MR. DIAFOIRUS [Feeling **ARGAN'S** pulse]
Now, Thomas, take the other arm of the gentleman, so that I may see whether you can form a right judgment on his pulse. Quid dicis?

THOMAS DIAFOIRUS
Dico that the pulse of this gentleman is the pulse of a man who is not well.

MR. DIAFOIRUS
Good.

THOMAS DIAFOIRUS
That it is duriusculus, not to say durus.

MR. DIAFOIRUS
Very well.

THOMAS DIAFOIRUS
Irregular.

MR. DIAFOIRUS
Bene.

THOMAS DIAFOIRUS
And even a little caprizant.

MR. DIAFOIRUS
Optime.

THOMAS DIAFOIRUS
Which speaks of an intemperance in the splenetic parenchyma; that is to say, the spleen.

MR. DIAFOIRUS
Quite right.

ARGAN

It cannot be, for Mr. Purgon says that it is my liver which is out of order.

MR. DIAFOIRUS

Certainly; he who says parenchyma says both one and the other, because of the great sympathy which exists between them through the means of the vas breve, of the pylorus, and often of the meatus choledici. He no doubt orders you to eat plenty of roast-meat.

ARGAN

No; nothing but boiled meat.

MR. DIAFOIRUS

Yes, yes; roast or boiled, it is all the same; he orders very wisely, and you could not have fallen into better hands.

ARGAN

Sir, tell me how many grains of salt I ought to put to an egg?

MR. DIAFOIRUS

Six, eight, ten, by even numbers; just as in medicines by odd numbers.

ARGAN

Good-bye, Sir; I hope soon to have the pleasure of seeing you again.

SCENE X

BÉLINE, ARGAN.

BÉLINE

Before I go out, I must inform you of one thing you must be careful about. While passing before Angélique's door, I saw with her a young man, who ran away as soon as he noticed me.

ARGAN

A young man with my daughter!

BÉLINE

Yes; your little girl Louison, who was with them, will tell you all about it.

ARGAN

Send her here, my love, send her here at once. Ah! the brazen-faced girl!
[Alone]
I no longer wonder at the resistance she showed.

SCENE XI

ARGAN, LOUISON.

LOUISON
What do you want, papa? My step-mamma told me to come to you.

ARGAN
Yes; come here. Come nearer. Turn round, and hold up your head. Look straight at me. Well?

LOUISON
What, papa?

ARGAN
So?

LOUISON
What?

ARGAN
Have you nothing to say to me?

LOUISON
Yes. I will, to amuse you, tell you, if you like, the story of the Ass's Skin or the fable of the Fox and the Crow, which I have learnt lately.

ARGAN
That is not what I want of you.

LOUISON
What is it then?

ARGAN
Ah! cunning little girl, you know very well what I mean.

LOUISON
No indeed, papa.

ARGAN
Is that the way you obey me?

LOUISON
What, papa?

ARGAN
Have I not asked you to tell me at once all you see?

LOUISON
Yes, papa.

ARGAN
Have you done so?

LOUISON
Yes, papa. I always come and tell you all I see.

ARGAN
And have you seen nothing to-day?

LOUISON
No, papa.

ARGAN
No?

LOUISON
No, papa.

ARGAN
Quite sure?

LOUISON
Quite sure.

ARGAN
Ah! indeed! I will make you see something soon.

LOUISON [Seeing **ARGAN** take a rod]
Ah! papa!

ARGAN
Ah! ah! false little girl; you do not tell me that you saw a man in your sister's room!

LOUISON [Crying]
Papa!

ARGAN [Taking **LOUISON** by the arm]
This will teach you to tell falsehoods.

LOUISON [Throwing herself on her knees]
Ah! my dear papa! pray forgive me. My sister had asked me not to say anything to you, but I will tell you everything.

ARGAN
First you must have a flogging for having told an untruth, then we will see to the rest.

LOUISON

Forgive me, papa, forgive me!

ARGAN
No, no!

LOUISON
My dear papa, don't whip me.

ARGAN
Yes, you shall be whipped.

LOUISON
For pity's sake! don't whip me, papa.

ARGAN [Going to whip her]
Come, come.

LOUISON
Ah! papa, you have hurt me; I am dead!

[She feigns to be dead.

ARGAN
How, now! What does this mean? Louison! Louison! Ah! heaven! Louison! My child! Ah! wretched father! My poor child is dead! What have I done? Ah! villainous rod! A curse on the rod! Ah! my poor child! My dear little Louison!

LOUISON
Come, come, dear papa; don't weep so. I am not quite dead yet.

ARGAN
Just see the cunning little wench. Well! I forgive you this once, but you must tell me everything.

LOUISON
Oh yes, dear papa.

ARGAN
Be sure you take great care, for here is my little finger that knows everything, and it will tell me if you don't speak the truth.

LOUISON
But, papa, you won't tell sister that I told you.

ARGAN
No, no.

LOUISON [After having listened to see if any one can hear]
Papa, a young man came into sister's room while I was there.

ARGAN
Well?

LOUISON
I asked him what he wanted; he said that he was her music-master.

ARGAN [Aside]
Hm! hm! I see.
[To **LOUISON**]
Well?

LOUISON
Then sister came.

ARGAN
Well?

LOUISON
She said to him, "Go away, go away, go. Good heavens! you will drive me to despair."

ARGAN
Well?

LOUISON
But he would not go away.

ARGAN
What did he say to her?

LOUISON
Oh! ever so many things.

ARGAN
But what?

LOUISON
He told her this, and that, and the other; that he loved her dearly; that she was the most beautiful person in the world.

ARGAN
And then, after?

LOUISON
Then he knelt down before her.

ARGAN
And then?

LOUISON

Then he kept on kissing her hands.

ARGAN

And then?

LOUISON

Then my mamma came to the door, and, he escaped.

ARGAN

Nothing else?

LOUISON

No, dear papa.

ARGAN

Here is my little finger, which says something though.

[Putting his finger up to his ear.

Wait. Stay, eh? ah! ah! Yes? oh! oh! here is my little finger, which says that there is something you saw, and which you do not tell me.

LOUISON

Ah! papa, your little finger is a story-teller.

ARGAN

Take care.

LOUISON

No, don't believe him; he tells a story, I assure you.

ARGAN

Oh! Well, well; we will see to that. Go away now, and pay great attention to what you see.
[Alone]
Ah! children are no longer children nowadays! What trouble! I have not even enough leisure to attend to my illness. I am quite done up.

[He falls down into his chair.

SCENE XII

BÉRALDE, ARGAN.

BÉRALDE

Well, brother! What is the matter? How are you?

ARGAN
Ah! very bad, brother; very bad.

BÉRALDE
How is that?

ARGAN
No one would believe how very feeble I am.

BÉRALDE
That's a sad thing, indeed.

ARGAN
I have hardly enough strength to speak.

BÉRALDE
I came here, brother, to propose a match for my niece, Angélique.

ARGAN [In a rage, speaking with great fury, and starting up from his chair]
Brother, don't speak to me of that wicked, good-for-nothing, insolent, brazen-faced girl. I will put her in a convent before two days are over.

BÉRALDE
Ah! all right! I am glad to see that you have a little strength still left, and that my visit does you good. Well, well, we will talk of business by-and-by. I have brought you an entertainment, which will dissipate your melancholy, and will dispose you better for what we have to talk about. They are gipsies dressed in Moorish clothes. They perform some dances mixed with songs, which, I am sure, you will like, and which will be as good as a prescription from Mr. Purgon. Come along.

SECOND INTERLUDE

MEN and **WOMEN** [Dressed as Moors]

FIRST MOORISH WOMAN.
When blooms the spring of life,
The golden harvest reap.
Waste not your years in bootless strife,
Till age upon your bodies creep.
But now, when shines the kindly light,
Give up your soul to love's delight.

No touch of sweetest joy
This longing heart can know,
No bliss without alloy

When love does silent show.

Then up, ye lads and lasses gay!
The spring of life is fair;
Cloud not these hours with care,
For love must win the day.

Beauty fades,
Years roll by,
Lowering shades
Obscure the sky.
And joys so sweet of yore
Shall charm us then no more.

Then up, ye lads and lasses gay!
The spring of life is fair;
Cloud not these hours with care,
For love must win the day.

FIRST ENTRY OF THE BALLET

2ND MOORISH WOMAN
They bid us love, they bid us woo,
Why seek delay?
To tender sighs and kisses too
In youth's fair day,
Our hearts are but too true.

The sweetest charms has Cupid's spell.
No sooner felt, the ready heart
His conquered self would yield him well
Ere yet the god had winged his dart.
But yet the tale we often hear
Of tears and sorrows keen,
To share in them, I ween,
Though sweet, would make us fear!

3RD MOORISH WOMAN
To love a lover true,
In youth's kind day, I trow,
Is pleasant task enow;
But think how we must rue
If he inconstant show!

4TH MOORISH WOMAN
The loss of lover false to me
But trifling grief would be,

Yet this is far the keenest smart
That he had stol'n away our heart.

2ND MOORISH WOMAN
What then shall we do
Whose hearts are so young?

4TH MOORISH WOMAN
Though cruel his laws,
Attended by woes,
Away with your arms,
Submit to his charms!

TOGETHER
His whims ye must follow,
His transports though fleet,
His pinings too sweet
Though often comes sorrow,
The thousand delights
The wounds of his darts
Still charm all the hearts.

ACT III

SCENE I

BÉRALDE, ARGAN, TOINETTE.

BÉRALDE
Well, brother, what do you say to that? Isn't it as good as a dose of cassia?

TOINETTE
Oh! good cassia is a very good thing, Sir.

BÉRALDE
Now, shall we have a little chat together.

ARGAN
Wait a moment, brother, I'll be back directly.

TOINETTE
Here, Sir; you forget that you cannot get about without a stick.

ARGAN
Ay, to be sure.

BÉRALDE, TOINETTE.

TOINETTE
Pray, do not give up the interest of your niece.

BÉRALDE
No, I shall do all in my power to forward her wishes.

TOINETTE
We must prevent this foolish marriage which he has got into his head, from taking place. And I thought to myself that it would be a good thing to introduce a doctor here, having a full understanding of our wishes, to disgust him with his Mr. Purgon, and abuse his mode of treating him. But as we have nobody to act that part for us, I have decided upon playing him a trick of my own.

BÉRALDE
In what way?

TOINETTE
It is rather an absurd idea, and it may be more fortunate than good. But act your own part. Here is our man.

SCENE III

ARGAN, BÉRALDE.

BÉRALDE
Let me ask you, brother, above all things not to excite yourself during our conversation.

ARGAN
I agree.

BÉRALDE
To answer without anger to anything I may mention.

ARGAN
Very well.

BÉRALDE
And to reason together upon the business I want to discuss with you without any irritation.

ARGAN
Dear me! Yes. What a preamble!

BÉRALDE

How is it, brother, that, with all the wealth you possess, and with only one daughter—for I do not count the little one—you speak of sending her to a convent?

ARGAN

How is it, brother, that I am master of my family, and that I can do all I think fit?

BÉRALDE

Your wife doesn't fail to advise you to get rid, in that way, of your two daughters; and I have no doubt that, through a spirit of charity, she would be charmed to see them both good nuns.

ARGAN

Oh, I see! My poor wife again! It is she who does all the harm, and everybody is against her.

BÉRALDE

No, brother; let us leave that alone. She is a woman with the best intentions in the world for the good of your family, and is free from all interested motives. She expresses for you the most extraordinary tenderness, and shows towards your children an inconceivable goodness. No, don't let us speak of her, but only of your daughter. What can be your reason for wishing to give her in marriage to the sort of a doctor?

ARGAN

My reason is that I wish to have a son-in-law who will suit my wants.

BÉRALDE

But it is not what your daughter requires, and we have a more suitable match for her.

ARGAN

Yes; but this one is more suitable for me.

BÉRALDE

But does she marry a husband for herself or for you, brother?

ARGAN

He must do both for her and for me, brother; and I wish to take into my family people of whom I have need.

BÉRALDE

So that, if your little girl were old enough, you would give her to an apothecary?

ARGAN

Why not?

BÉRALDE

Is it possible that you should always be so infatuated with your apothecaries and doctors, and be so determined to be ill, in spite of men and nature?

ARGAN

What do you mean by that, brother?

BÉRALDE

I mean, brother, that I know of no man less sick than you, and that I should be quite satisfied with a constitution no worse than yours. One great proof that you are well, and that you have a body perfectly well made, is that with all the pains you have taken, you have failed as yet in injuring the soundness of your constitution, and that you have not died of all the medicine they have made you swallow.

ARGAN

But are you aware, brother, that it is these medicines which keep me in good health? Mr. Purgon says that I should go off if he were but three days without taking care of me.

BÉRALDE

If you are not careful, he will take such care of you that he will soon send you into the next world.

ARGAN

But let us reason together, brother; don't you believe at all in medicine?

BÉRALDE

No, brother; and I do not see that it is necessary for our salvation to believe in it.

ARGAN

What! Do you not hold true a thing acknowledged by everybody, and revered throughout all ages?

BÉRALDE

Between ourselves, far from thinking it true, I look upon it as one of the greatest follies which exist among men; and to consider things from a philosophical point of view, I don't know of a more absurd piece of mummery, of anything more ridiculous, than a man who takes upon himself to cure another man.

ARGAN

Why will you not believe that a man can cure another?

BÉRALDE

For the simple reason, brother, that the springs of our machines are mysteries about which men are as yet completely in the dark, and nature has put too thick a veil before our eyes for us to know anything about it.

ARGAN

Then, according to you, the doctors know nothing at all.

BÉRALDE

Oh yes, brother. Most of them have some knowledge of the best classics, can talk fine Latin, can give a Greek name to every disease, can define and distinguish them; but as to curing these diseases, that's out of the question.

ARGAN

Still, you must agree to this, that doctors know more than others.

BÉRALDE
They know, brother, what I have told you; and that does not effect many cures. All the excellency of their art consists in pompous gibberish, in a specious babbling, which gives you words instead of reasons, and promises instead Of results.

ARGAN
Still, brother, there exist men as wise and clever as you, and we see that in cases of illness every one has recourse to the doctor.

BÉRALDE
It is a proof of human weakness, and not of the truth of their art.

ARGAN
Still, doctors must believe in their art, since they make use of it for themselves.

BÉRALDE
It is because some of them share the popular error by which they themselves profit, while others profit by it without sharing it. Your Mr. Purgon has no wish to deceive; he is a thorough doctor from head to foot, a man who believes in his rules more than in all the demonstrations of mathematics, and who would think it a crime to question them. He sees nothing obscure in physic, nothing doubtful, nothing difficult, and through an impetuous prepossession, an obstinate confidence, a coarse common sense and reason, orders right and left purgatives and bleedings, and hesitates at nothing. We must bear him no ill-will for the harm he does us; it is with the best intentions in the world that he will send you into the next world, and in killing you he will do no more than he has done to his wife and children, and than he would do to himself, if need be.[4]

ARGAN
It is because you have a spite against him. But let us come to the point. What is to be done when one is ill?

BÉRALDE
Nothing, brother.

ARGAN
Nothing?

BÉRALDE
Nothing. Only rest. Nature, when we leave her free, will herself gently recover from the disorder into which she has fallen. It is our anxiety, our impatience, which does the mischief, and most men die of their remedies, and not of their diseases.

ARGAN
Still you must acknowledge, brother, that we can in certain things help nature.

BÉRALDE

Alas! brother; these are pure fancies, with which we deceive ourselves. At all times, there have crept among men brilliant fancies in which we believe, because they flatter us, and because it would be well if they were true. When a doctor speaks to us of assisting, succouring nature, of removing what is injurious to it, of giving it what it is defective in, of restoring it, and giving back to it the full exercise of its functions, when he speaks of purifying the blood, of refreshing the bowels and the brain, of correcting the spleen, of rebuilding the lungs, of renovating the liver, of fortifying the heart, of re-establishing and keeping up the natural heat, and of possessing secrets wherewith to lengthen life of many years—he repeats to you the romance of physic. But when you test the truth of what he has promised to you, you find that it all ends in nothing; it is like those beautiful dreams which only leave you in the morning the regret of having believed in them.

ARGAN

Which means that all the knowledge of the world is contained in your brain, and that you think you know more than all the great doctors of our age put together.

BÉRALDE

When you weigh words and actions, your great doctors are two different kinds of people. Listen to their talk, they are the cleverest people in the world; see them at work, and they are the most ignorant.

ARGAN

Heyday! You are a great doctor, I see, and I wish that some one of those gentlemen were here to take up your arguments and to check your babble.

BÉRALDE

I do not take upon myself, brother, to fight against physic; and every one at their own risk and peril may believe what he likes. What I say is only between ourselves; and I should have liked, in order to deliver you from the error into which you have fallen, and in order to amuse you, to take you to see some of Molière's comedies on this subject.

ARGAN

Your Molière is a fine impertinent fellow with his comedies! I think it mightily pleasant of him to go and take off honest people like the doctors.

BÉRALDE

It is not the doctors themselves that he takes off, but the absurdity of medicine.

ARGAN

It becomes him well, truly, to control the faculty! He's a nice simpleton, and a nice impertinent fellow to laugh at consultations and prescriptions, to attack the body of physicians, and to bring on his stage such venerable people as those gentlemen.

BÉRALDE

What would you have him bring there but the different professions of men? Princes and kings are brought there every day, and they are of as good a stock as your physicians.

ARGAN

No, by all the devils! if I were a physician, I would be revenged of his impertinence, and when he falls ill, I would let him die without relief. In vain would he beg and pray. I would not prescribe for him the least little bleeding, the least little injection, and I would tell him, "Die, die, like a dog; it will teach you to laugh at us doctors."

BÉRALDE
You are terribly angry with him.

ARGAN
Yes, he is an ill-advised fellow, and if the doctors are wise, they will do what I say.

BÉRALDE
He will be wiser than the doctors, for he will not go and ask their help.

ARGAN
So much the worse for him, if he has not recourse to their remedies.

BÉRALDE
He has his reasons for not wishing to have anything to do with them; he is certain that only strong and robust constitutions can bear their remedies in addition to the illness, and he has only just enough strength for his sickness.

ARGAN
What absurd reasons. Here, brother, don't speak to me anymore about that man; for it makes me savage, and you will give me his complaint.

BÉRALDE
I will willingly cease, brother; and, to change the subject, allow me to tell you that, because your daughter shows a slight repugnance to the match you propose, it is no reason why you should shut her up in a convent. In your choice of a son-in-law you should not blindly follow the anger which masters you. We should in such a matter yield a little to the inclinations of a daughter, since it is for all her life, and the whole happiness of her married life depends on it.

SCENE IV

MR. FLEURANT, ARGAN, BÉRALDE.

ARGAN
Ah! brother, with your leave.

BÉRALDE
Eh? What are you going to do?

ARGAN
To take this little clyster; it will soon be done.

BÉRALDE

Are you joking? Can you not spend one moment without clysters or physic? Put it off to another time, and be quiet.

ARGAN

Mr. Fleurant, let it be for to-night or to-morrow morning.

MR. FLEURANT [To **BÉRALDE**]

What right have you to interfere? How dare you oppose yourself to the prescription of the doctors, and prevent the gentleman from taking my clyster? You are a nice fellow to show such boldness.

BÉRALDE

Go, Sir, go; it is easy to see that you are not accustomed to speak face to face with men.

MR. FLEURANT

You ought not thus to sneer at physic, and make me lose my precious time. I came here for a good prescription, and I will go and tell Mr. Purgon that I have been prevented from executing his orders, and that I have been stopped in the performance of my duty. You'll see, you'll see....

SCENE V

ARGAN, BÉRALDE.

ARGAN

Brother, you'll be the cause that some misfortune will happen here.

BÉRALDE

What a misfortune not to take a clyster prescribed by Mr. Purgon! Once more, brother, is it possible that you can't be cured of this doctor disease, and that you will thus bring yourself under their remedies?

ARGAN

Ah! brother. You speak like a man who is quite well, but if you were in my place, you would soon change your way of speaking. It is easy to speak against medicine when one is in perfect health.

BÉRALDE

But what disease do you suffer from?

ARGAN

You will drive me to desperation. I should like you to have my disease, and then we should see if you would prate as you do. Ah! here is Mr. Purgon.

SCENE VI

MR. PURGON, ARGAN, BÉRALDE, TOINETTE.

MR. PURGON
I have just heard nice news downstairs! You laugh at my prescriptions, and refuse to take the remedy which I ordered.

ARGAN
Sir, it is not....

MR. PURGON
What daring boldness, what a strange revolt of a patient against his doctor!

TOINETTE
It is frightful.

MR. PURGON
A clyster which I have had the pleasure of composing myself.

ARGAN
It was not I....

MR. PURGON
Invented and made up according to all the rules of art.

TOINETTE
He was wrong.

MR. PURGON
And which was to work a marvellous effect on the intestines.

ARGAN
My brother....

MR. PURGON
To send it back with contempt!

ARGAN [Showing **BÉRALDE**]
It was he....

MR. PURGON
Such conduct is monstrous.

TOINETTE
So it is.

MR. PURGON
It is a fearful outrage against medicine.

ARGAN [Showing **BÉRALDE**]
He is the cause....

MR. PURGON
A crime of high-treason against the faculty, and one which cannot be too severely punished.

TOINETTE
You are quite right.

MR. PURGON
I declare to you that I break off all intercourse with you.

ARGAN
It is my brother....

MR. PURGON
That I will have no more connection with you.

TOINETTE
You will do quite right.

MR. PURGON
And to end all association with you, here is the deed of gift which I made to my nephew in favour of the marriage.

[He tears the document, and throws the pieces about furiously.

ARGAN
It is my brother who has done all the mischief.

MR. PURGON
To despise my clyster!

ARGAN
Let it be brought, I will take it directly.

MR. PURGON
I would have cured you in a very short time.

TOINETTE
He doesn't deserve it.

MR. PURGON
I was about to cleanse your body, and to clear it of its bad humours.

ARGAN
Ah! my brother!

MR. PURGON
And it wanted only a dozen purgatives to cleanse it entirely.

TOINETTE
He is unworthy of your care.

MR. PURGON
But since you would not be cured by me....

ARGAN
It was not my fault.

MR. PURGON
Since you have forsaken the obedience you owe to your doctor....

TOINETTE
It cries for vengeance.

MR. PURGON
Since you have declared yourself a rebel against the remedies I had prescribed for you....

ARGAN
No, no, certainly not.

MR. PURGON
I must now tell you that I give you up to your bad constitution, to the imtemperament of your intestines, to the corruption of your blood, to the acrimony of your bile, and to the feculence of your humours.

TOINETTE
It serves you right.

ARGAN
Alas!

MR. PURGON
And I will have you before four days in an incurable state.

ARGAN
Ah! mercy on me!

MR. PURGON
You shall fall into bradypepsia.

ARGAN
Mr. Purgon!

MR. PURGON
From bradypepsia into dyspepsia.

ARGAN

Mr. Purgon!

MR. PURGON
From dyspepsia into apepsy.

ARGAN
Mr. Purgon!

MR. PURGON
From apepsy into lientery.

ARGAN
Mr. Purgon!

MR. PURGON
From lientery into dysentery.

ARGAN
Mr. Purgon!

MR. PURGON
From dysentery into dropsy.

ARGAN
Mr. Purgon!

MR. PURGON
And from dropsy to the deprivation of life into which your folly will bring you.

SCENE VII

ARGAN, BÉRALDE.

ARGAN
Ah heaven! I am dead. Brother, you have undone me.

BÉRALDE
Why? What is the matter?

ARGAN
I am undone. I feel already that the faculty is avenging itself.

BÉRALDE
Really, brother, you are crazy, and I would not for a great deal that you should be seen acting as you are doing. Shake yourself a little, I beg, recover yourself, and do not give way so much to your imagination.

ARGAN

You hear, brother, with what strange diseases he has threatened me.

BÉRALDE

What a foolish fellow you are!

ARGAN

He says that I shall become incurable within four days.

BÉRALDE

And what does it signify what he says? Is it an oracle that has spoken? To hear you, anyone would think that Mr. Purgon holds in his hands the thread of your life, and that he has supreme authority to prolong it or to cut it short at his will. Remember that the springs of your life are in yourself, and that all the wrath of Mr. Purgon can do as little towards making you die, as his remedies can do to make you live. This is an opportunity, if you like to take it, of getting rid of your doctors; and if you are so constituted that you cannot do without them, it is easy for you, brother, to have another with whom you run less risk.

ARGAN

Ah, brother! he knows all about my constitution, and the way to treat me.

BÉRALDE

I must acknowledge that you are greatly infatuated, and that you look at things with strange eyes.

SCENE VIII

ARGAN, TOINETTE, BÉRALDE.

TOINETTE [To **ARGAN**]

There is a doctor, here, Sir, who desires to see you.

ARGAN

What doctor?

TOINETTE

A doctor of medicine.

ARGAN

I ask you who he is?

TOINETTE

I don't know who he is, but he is as much like me as two peas, and if I was not sure that my mother was an honest woman, I should say that this is a little brother she has given me since my father's death.

SCENE IX

ARGAN, BÉRALDE.

BÉRALDE
You are served according to your wish. One doctor leaves you, another comes to replace him.

ARGAN
I greatly fear that you will cause some misfortune.

BÉRALDE
Oh! You are harping upon that string again?

ARGAN
Ah! I have on my mind all those diseases that I don't understand, those ...

SCENE X

ARGAN, BÉRALDE, TOINETTE dressed as a doctor.

TOINETTE
Allow me, Sir, to come and pay my respects to you, and to offer you my small services for all the bleedings and purging you may require.

ARGAN
I am much obliged to you, Sir.
[To **BÉRALDE**]
Toinette herself, I declare!

TOINETTE
I beg you will excuse me one moment, Sir. I forgot to give a small order to my servant.

SCENE XI

ARGAN, BÉRALDE.

ARGAN
Would you not say that this is really Toinette?

BÉRALDE
It is true that the resemblance is very striking. But it is not the first time that we have seen this kind of thing, and history is full of those freaks of nature.

ARGAN

For my part, I am astonished, and ...

SCENE XII

ARGAN, BÉRALDE, TOINETTE.

TOINETTE
What do you want, Sir?

ARGAN
What?

TOINETTE
Did you not call me?

ARGAN
I? No.

TOINETTE
My ears must have tingled then.

ARGAN
Just stop here one moment and see how much that doctor is like you.

TOINETTE
Ah! yes, indeed, I have plenty of time to waste! Besides, I have seen enough of him already.

SCENE XIII

ARGAN, BÉRALDE.

ARGAN
Had I not seen them both together, I should have believed it was one and the same person.

BÉRALDE
I have read wonderful stories about such resemblances; and we have seen some in our day that have taken in everybody.

ARGAN
For my part, I should have been deceived this time, and sworn that the two were but one.

SCENE XIV

ARGAN, BÉRALDE, TOINETTE as a doctor.

TOINETTE
Sir, I beg your pardon with all my heart.

ARGAN [To **BÉRALDE**]
It is wonderful.

TOINETTE
You will not take amiss, I hope, the curiosity I feel to see such an illustrious patient; and your reputation, which reaches the farthest ends of the world, must be my excuse for the liberty I am taking.

ARGAN
Sir, I am your servant.

TOINETTE
I see, Sir, that you are looking earnestly at me. What age do you think I am?

ARGAN
I should think twenty-six or twenty-seven at the utmost.

TOINETTE
Ah! ah! ah! ah! ah! I am ninety years old.

ARGAN
Ninety years old!

TOINETTE
Yes; this is what the secrets of my art have done for me to preserve me fresh and vigorous as you see.

ARGAN
Upon my word, a fine youthful old fellow of ninety!

TOINETTE
I am an itinerant doctor, and go from town to town, from province to province, from kingdom to kingdom, to seek out illustrious material for my abilities; to find patients worthy of my attention, capable of exercising the great and noble secrets which I have discovered in medicine. I disdain to amuse myself with the small rubbish of common diseases, with the trifles of rheumatism, coughs, fevers, vapours, and headaches. I require diseases of importance, such as good non-intermittent fevers with delirium, good scarlet-fevers, good plagues, good confirmed dropsies, good pleurisies with inflammations of the lungs. These are what I like, what I triumph in, and I wish, Sir, that you had all those diseases combined, that you had been given up, despaired of by all the doctors, and at the point of death, so that I might have the pleasure of showing you the excellency of my remedies, and the desire I have of doing you service!

ARGAN
I am greatly obliged to you, Sir, for the kind intentions you have towards me.

TOINETTE

Let me feel your pulse. Come, come, beat properly, please. Ah! I will soon make you beat as you should. This pulse is trifling with me; I see that it does not know me yet. Who is your doctor?

ARGAN

Mr. Purgon.

TOINETTE

That man is not noted in my books among the great doctors. What does he say you are ill of?

ARGAN

He says it is the liver, and others say it is the spleen.

TOINETTE

They are a pack of ignorant blockheads; you are suffering from the lungs.

ARGAN

The lungs?

TOINETTE

Yes; what do you feel?

ARGAN

From time to time great pains in my head.

TOINETTE

Just so; the lungs.

ARGAN

At times it seems as if I had a mist before my eyes.

TOINETTE

The lungs.

ARGAN

I feel sick now and then.

TOINETTE

The lungs.

ARGAN

And I feel sometimes a weariness in all my limbs.

TOINETTE

The lungs.

ARGAN

And sometimes I have sharp pains in the stomach, as if I had the colic.

TOINETTE
The lungs. Do you eat your food with appetite?

ARGAN
Yes, Sir.

TOINETTE
The lungs. Do you like to drink a little wine?

ARGAN
Yes, Sir.

TOINETTE
The lungs. You feel sleepy after your meals, and willingly enjoy a nap?

ARGAN
Yes, Sir.

TOINETTE
The lungs, the lungs, I tell you. What does your doctor order you for food?

ARGAN
He orders me soup.

TOINETTE
Ignoramus!

ARGAN
Fowl.

TOINETTE
Ignoramus!

ARGAN
Veal.

TOINETTE
Ignoramus!

ARGAN
Broth.

TOINETTE
Ignoramus!

ARGAN

New-laid eggs.

TOINETTE
Ignoramus!

ARGAN
And at night a few prunes to relax the bowels.

TOINETTE
Ignoramus!

ARGAN
And, above all, to drink my wine well diluted with water.

TOINETTE
Ignorantus, ignoranta, ignorantum. You must drink your wine pure; and to thicken your blood, which is too thin, you must eat good fat beef, good fat pork, good Dutch cheese, some gruel, rice puddings, chestnuts, and thin cakes,[5] to make all adhere and conglutinate. Your doctor is an ass. I will send you one of my own school, and will come and examine you from time to time during my stay in this town.

ARGAN
You will oblige me greatly.

TOINETTE
What the deuce do you want with this arm?

ARGAN
What?

TOINETTE
If I were you, I should have it cut off on the spot.

ARGAN
Why?

TOINETTE
Don't you see that it attracts all the nourishment to itself, and hinders this side from growing?

ARGAN
May be; but I have need of my arm.

TOINETTE
You have also a right eye that I would have plucked out if I were in your place.

ARGAN
My right eye plucked out?

TOINETTE

Don't you see that it interferes with the other, and robs it of its nourishment? Believe me; have it plucked out as soon as possible; you will see all the clearer with the left eye.

ARGAN
There is no need to hurry.

TOINETTE
Good-bye. I am sorry to leave you so soon, but I must assist at a grand consultation which is to take place about a man who died yesterday.

ARGAN
About a man who died yesterday?

TOINETTE
Yes, that we may consider and see what ought to have been done to cure him. Good-bye.

ARGAN
You know that patients do not use ceremony.

SCENE XV

ARGAN, BÉRALDE.

BÉRALDE
Upon my word, this doctor seems to be a very clever man.

ARGAN
Yes, but he goes a little too fast.

BÉRALDE
All great doctors do so.

ARGAN
Cut off my arm and pluck out my eye, so that the other may be better. I had rather that it were not better. A nice operation indeed, to make me at once one-eyed and one-armed.

SCENE XVI

ARGAN, BÉRALDE, TOINETTE.

TOINETTE [Pretending to speak to somebody]
Come, come, I am your servant; I'm in no joking humour.

ARGAN

What is the matter?

TOINETTE
Your doctor, forsooth, who wanted to feel my pulse!

ARGAN
Just imagine; and that, too, at fourscore and ten years of age.

BÉRALDE
Now, I say, brother, since you have quarrelled with Mr. Purgon, won't you give me leave to speak of the match which is proposed for my niece?

ARGAN
No, brother; I will put her in a convent, since she has rebelled against me. I see plainly that there is some love business at the bottom of it all, and I have discovered a certain secret interview which they don't suspect me to know anything about.

BÉRALDE
Well, brother, and suppose there were some little inclination, where could the harm be? Would it be so criminal when it all tends to what is honourable—marriage?

ARGAN
Be that as it may, she will be a nun. I have made up my mind.

BÉRALDE
You intend to please somebody by so doing.

ARGAN
I understand what you mean. You always come back to that, and my wife is very much in your way.

BÉRALDE
Well, yes, brother; since I must speak out, it is your wife I mean; for I can no more bear with your infatuation about doctors than with your infatuation about your wife, and see you run headlong into every snare she lays for you.

TOINETTE
Ah! Sir, don't talk so of mistress. She is a person against whom there is nothing to be said; a woman without deceit, and who loves master—ah! who loves him.... I can't express how much.

ARGAN [To **BÉRALDE**]
Just ask her all the caresses she lavishes for me.

TOINETTE
Yes, indeed!

ARGAN
And all the uneasiness my sickness causes her.

TOINETTE
Certainly.

ARGAN
And the care and trouble she takes about me.

TOINETTE
Quite right.
[To **BÉRALDE**]
Will you let me convince you; and to show you at once how my mistress loves my master.
[To **ARGAN**]
Sir, allow me to undeceive him, and to show him his mistake.

ARGAN
How?

TOINETTE
My mistress will soon come back. Stretch yourself full-length in this arm-chair, and pretend to be dead. You will see what grief she will be in when I tell her the news.

ARGAN
Very well, I consent.

TOINETTE
Yes; but don't leave her too long in despair, for she might die of it.

ARGAN
Trust me for that.

TOINETTE [To **BÉRALDE**]
Hide yourself in that corner.

SCENE XVII

ARGAN, TOINETTE.

ARGAN
Is there no danger in counterfeiting death?

TOINETTE
No, no. What danger can there be? Only stretch yourself there. It will be so pleasant to put your brother to confusion. Here is my mistress. Mind you keep still.

SCENE XVIII

BÉLINE, ARGAN stretched out in his chair, **TOINETTE.**

TOINETTE [Pretending not to see **BÉLINE**]
Ah heavens! Ah! what a misfortune! What a strange accident!

BÉLINE
What is the matter, Toinette?

TOINETTE
Ah! Madam!

BÉLINE
What ails you?

TOINETTE
Your husband is dead.

BÉLINE
My husband is dead?

TOINETTE
Alas! yes; the poor soul is gone.

BÉLINE
Are you quite certain?

TOINETTE
Quite certain. Nobody knows of it yet. I was all alone here when it happened. He has just breathed his last in my arms. Here, just look at him, full-length in his chair.

BÉLINE
Heaven be praised. I am delivered from a most grievous burden. How silly of you, Toinette, to be so afflicted at his death.

TOINETTE
Ah! Ma'am, I thought I ought to cry.

BÉLINE
Pooh! it is not worth the trouble. What loss is it to anybody, and what good did he do in this world? A wretch, unpleasant to everybody; of nauseous, dirty habits; always a clyster or a dose of physic in his body. Always snivelling, coughing, spitting; a stupid, tedious, ill-natured fellow, who was for ever fatiguing people and scolding night and day at his maids and servants.

TOINETTE
An excellent funeral oration!

BÉLINE

Toinette, you must help me to carry out my design; and you may depend upon it that I will make it worth your while if you serve me. Since, by good luck, nobody is aware of his death, let us put him into his bed, and keep the secret until I have done what I want. There are some papers and some money I must possess myself of. It is not right that I should have passed the best years of my life with him without any kind of advantage. Come along, Toinette, first of all, let us take all the keys.

ARGAN [Getting up hastily]
Softly.

BÉLINE
Ah!

ARGAN
So, my wife, it is thus you love me?

TOINETTE
Ah! the dead man is not dead.

ARGAN [To **BÉLINE**, who goes away]
I am very glad to see how you love me, and to have heard the noble panegyric you made upon me. This is a good warning, which will make me wise for the future, and prevent me from doing many things.

SCENE XIX

BÉRALDE coming out of the place where he was hiding, **ARGAN, TOINETTE.**

BÉRALDE
Well, brother, you see....

TOINETTE
Now, really, I could never have believed such a thing. But I hear your daughter coming, place yourself as you were just now, and let us see how she will receive the news. It is not a bad thing to try; and since you have begun, you will be able by this means to know the sentiments of your family towards you.

SCENE XX

ARGAN, ANGÉLIQUE, TOINETTE.

TOINETTE [Pretending not to see **ANGÉLIQUE**]
O heavens! what a sad accident! What an unhappy day!

ANGÉLIQUE
What ails you, Toinette, and why do you cry?

TOINETTE
Alas! I have such sad news for you.

ANGÉLIQUE
What is it?

TOINETTE
Your father is dead.

ANGÉLIQUE
My father is dead, Toinette?

TOINETTE
Yes, just look at him there; he died only a moment ago of a fainting fit that came over him.

ANGÉLIQUE
O heavens! what a misfortune! What a cruel grief! Alas! why must I lose my father, the only being left me in the world? and why should I lose him, too, at a time when he was angry with me? What will become of me, unhappy girl that I am? What consolation can I find after so great a loss?

SCENE XXI

ARGAN, ANGÉLIQUE, CLÉANTE, TOINETTE.

CLÉANTE
What is the matter with you, dear Angélique, and what misfortune makes you weep?

ANGÉLIQUE
Alas! I weep for what was most dear and most precious to me. I weep for the death of my father.

CLÉANTE
O heaven! what a misfortune! What an unforeseen stroke of fortune! Alas! after I had asked your uncle to ask you in marriage, I was coming to see him, in order to try by my respect and entreaties to incline his heart to grant you to my wishes.

ANGÉLIQUE
Ah! Cléante, let us talk no more of this. Let us give up all hopes of marriage. Now my father is dead, I will have nothing to do with the world, and will renounce it for ever. Yes, my dear father, if I resisted your will, I will at least follow out one of your intentions, and will by that make amends for the sorrow I have caused you.

[Kneeling.

Let me, father, make you this promise here, and kiss you as a proof of my repentance.

ARGAN [Kissing **ANGÉLIQUE**]

Ah! my daughter!

ANGÉLIQUE
Ah!

ARGAN
Come; do not be afraid. I am not dead. Ah! you are my true flesh and blood and my real daughter; I am delighted to have discovered your good heart.

SCENE XXII

ARGAN, BÉRALDE, ANGÉLIQUE, CLÉANTE, TOINETTE.

ANGÉLIQUE
Ah! what a delightful surprise! Father, since heaven has given you back to our love, let me here throw myself at your feet to implore one favour of you. If you do not approve of what my heart feels, if you refuse to give me Cléante for a husband, I conjure you, at least, not to force me to marry another. It is all I have to ask of you.

CLÉANTE [Throwing himself at **ARGAN'S** feet]
Ah! Sir, allow your heart to be touched by her entreaties and by mine, and do not oppose our mutual love.

BÉRALDE
Brother, how can you resist all this?

TOINETTE
Will you remain insensible before such affection?

ARGAN
Well, let him become a doctor, and I will consent to the marriage.
[To **CLÉANTE**]
Yes, turn doctor, Sir, and I will give you my daughter.

CLÉANTE
Very willingly, Sir, if it is all that is required to become your son-in-law. I will turn doctor; apothecary also, if you like. It is not such a difficult thing after all, and I would do much more to obtain from you the fair Angélique.

BÉRALDE
But, brother, it just strikes me; why don't you turn doctor yourself? It would be much more convenient to have all you want within yourself.

TOINETTE
Quite true. That is the very way to cure yourself. There is no disease bold enough to dare to attack the person of a doctor.

ARGAN

I imagine, brother, that you are laughing at me. Can I study at my age?

BÉRALDE

Study! What need is there? You are clever enough for that; there are a great many who are not a bit more clever than you are.

ARGAN

But one must be able to speak Latin well, and know the different diseases and the remedies they require.

BÉRALDE

When you put on the cap and gown of a doctor, all that will come of itself, and you will afterwards be much more clever than you care to be.

ARGAN

What! We understand how to discourse upon diseases when we have that dress?

BÉRALDE

Yes; you have only to hold forth; when you have a cap and gown, any stuff becomes learned, and all rubbish good sense.

TOINETTE

Look you, Sir; a beard is something in itself; a beard is half the doctor.

CLÉANTE

Anyhow, I am ready for everything.

BÉRALDE [To **ARGAN**]

Shall we have the thing done immediately?

ARGAN

How, immediately?

BÉRALDE

Yes, in your house.

ARGAN

In my house?

BÉRALDE

Yes, I know a body of physicians, friends of mine, who will come presently, and will perform the ceremony in your hall. It will cost you nothing.

ARGAN

But what can I say, what can I answer?

BÉRALDE

You will be instructed in a few words, and they will give you in writing all you have to say. Go and dress yourself directly, and I will send for them.

ARGAN

Very well; let it be done.

SCENE XXIII

BÉRALDE, ANGÉLIQUE, CLÉANTE.

CLÉANTE

What is it yon intend to do, and what do you mean by this body of physicians?

TOINETTE

What is it you are going to do?

BÉRALDE

To amuse ourselves a little to-night. The players have made a doctor's admission the subject of an interlude, with dances and music. I want everyone to enjoy it, and my brother to act the principal part in it.

ANGÉLIQUE

But, uncle, it seems to me that you are making fun of my father.

BÉRALDE

But, niece, it is not making too much fun of him to fall in with his fancies. We may each of us take part in it ourselves, and thus perform the comedy for each other's amusement. Carnival time authorises it. Let us go quickly and get everything ready.

CLÉANTE [To **ANGÉLIQUE**]

Do you consent to it?

ANGÉLIQUE

Yes; since my uncle takes the lead.

FOOTNOTES:

[1] As usual, Argan only counts half; even after he has reduced the charge.

[2] Thomas Diafoirus is evidently going to base some compliment on the belle-mère. The only way out *of the difficulty in English seems to be to complete the sentence somewhat.*

[3] *Harvey's treatise on the circulation of the blood was published in 1628. His discovery was violently opposed for a long time afterwards.*

[4] Molière seems to refer to Dr. Guenaut, who was said to have killed with antimony (his favourite remedy) his wife, his daughter, his nephew, and two of his sons-in-law—AIMÉ MARTIN.

[5] Oubliés; now called plaisirs. "Wafers" would perhaps have been the right rendering in Molière's time.

[6] This piece is composed of a mixture of dog-Latin, French, &c. and is utterly untranslateable.

[7] It is said that it was when uttering this word that Molière gave way to the illness from which he had long suffered.

Molière – A Short Biography

Jean-Baptiste Poquelin is better known to us by his stage name of Molière. He was born in Paris, to a prosperous well-to-do family, the son of Jean Poquelin and Marie Cressé, on 15th January 1622.

It is said that a maid, seeing him for the first time shrieked, "Le nez!", a reference to the infant's large nose. The name stuck as a family nickname from that time. At ten his mother died and his relationship with his father seems to have been lukewarm at best.

It is probable that his education started with studies in a Parisian elementary school. This was followed with his enrolment in the prestigious Jesuit Collège de Clermont, where he completed his studies in a strict academic environment but also first sampled life on the stage.

In 1631, his father purchased from the court of Louis XIII the posts of "valet de chambre ordinaire et tapissier du Roi" ("valet of the King's chamber and keeper of carpets and upholstery").

Molière assumed his father's posts in 1641. The benefits included only three months' work per annum for which he was paid 300 livres and also provided a number of lucrative contracts.

To increase the spectrum of his skills Molière also studied as a provincial lawyer around 1642, probably in Orléans, but it is not recorded if he ever qualified. Up to this date he had followed his father's plans for a career and they had served him well; he seemed destined for a career in office.

However, in June 1643, when he was 21, Molière abandoned this path for his first love; a career on the stage. He partnered with the actress Madeleine Béjart, to found the Illustre Théâtre at a cost of 630 livres.

Unfortunately, despite their enthusiasm, effort and ambition the troupe went bankrupt in 1645. Molière, now in charge, due to both his acting prowess and his legal training, had run up debts, mainly for the rent of the theatre, of 2000 livres. Molière was thrown into prison. Historians differ as to who paid the debts but after a 24-hour stint in jail Molière returned to the acting circuit.

It was at this time that he began to use the pseudonym Molière. It may also have been to spare his father the shame of having an actor in the family; a lowly profession for his status in society.

Molière and Madeleine now began with a new group of actors and spent the next dozen years touring the provincial circuit. The company slowly gained in success. Molière was also writing much of what they acted. Sadly only a few plays survive from this period among them 'The Bungler' and 'The Doctor in Love'. They represent though a distinct move away from the Italian improvisational Commedia dell'arte and highlight his use of mockery.

Armand, Prince of Conti, the governor of Languedoc, now also became his patron in return the company was named after him. Sadly for Molière the friendship later ended when Conti, having contracted syphilis from a courtesan, turned towards religion and joined Molière's enemies in the Parti des Dévots and the Compagnie de Saint Sacrement.

Molière's' journey back to the sacred land of Parisian theatres was slow. However by 1658 he performed in front of the King at the Louvre (then a theatre for hire) in Corneille's tragedy 'Nicomède' and in the farce 'Le Docteur Amoureux' (The Doctor in Love) with some success. He was awarded the title of Troupe de Monsieur (Monsieur being the honorific for the king's brother Philippe I, Duke of Orléans). With the help of Monsieur, his company was allowed to share the theatre in the large hall of the Petit-Bourbon with the famous Italian Commedia dell'arte company of Tiberio Fiorillo. The companies performed in the theatre on alternate nights.

The premiere of Molière's 'Les Précieuses Ridicules' (The Affected Young Ladies) took place at the Petit-Bourbon on 18th November 1659. It was the first of Molière's many attempts to satirize certain societal mannerisms and affectations then common in France. It won Molière the attention and the criticism of many, but alas not a large audience. He then asked Fiorillo to teach him the techniques of Commedia dell'arte. His 1660 play 'Sganarelle, ou Le Cocu imaginaire' (The Imaginary Cuckold) seems to be a tribute both to Commedia dell'arte and to his teacher.

Despite his own preference for tragedy, Molière became famous for these farces, which were generally in one act and performed after the tragedy. Some of these farces were only partly written and performed in the style of Commedia dell'arte with improvisation over a sketched out plot. He also wrote two comedies in verse, but these were less successful.

In 1660 the Petit-Bourbon was demolished to make way for the expansion of the Louvre. Molière's company decamped to the abandoned theatre in the Palais-Royal which was in the process of being refurbished. The company opened there on 20th January 1661. In order to please his patron, Monsieur, who was so enthralled with the arts that he was soon excluded from state affairs, Molière wrote and played 'Dom Garcie de Navarre ou Le Prince jaloux' (The Jealous Prince, 4th February 1661), a heroic comedy derived from a work of Cicognini's. Two other comedies of the same year were the successful 'L'École des maris' (The School for Husbands) and 'Les Fâcheux', (The Mad also known as The Bores) subtitled Comédie faite pour les divertissements du Roi (a comedy for the King's amusements) as it was performed during a series of parties that Nicolas Fouquet gave in honor of the king. These entertainments led to the arrest of Fouquet for wasting public money. He was sentenced to life imprisonment.

In parallel with 'Les Fâcheux', Molière introduced the comédies-ballets. These ballets were a transitional form of dance performance between the court ballets of Louis XIV and the art of professional theatre which was developing rapidly with the use of the proscenium stage. The comédies-ballets developed by chance when Molière was enlisted to mount both a play and a ballet in the honor of Louis XIV and found that he did not have a large enough cast to meet the needs of both. Cleverly Molière decided to combine the ballet and the play to achieve his goals. The gamble paid off handsomely. Molière was asked to produce twelve more comédies-ballets before his death. During these Molière collaborated with Pierre Beauchamp. Beauchamp codified the five balletic positions of the feet and arms and was partly responsible for the creation of the Beauchamp-Feuillet dance notation. He also collaborated with Jean-Baptiste Lully, a dancer, choreographer, and composer, whose reign at the Paris Opéra ran for fifteen years. Under Molière's command, ballet and opera became professional arts unto themselves. The comédies-ballets closely integrated dance with music and the action of the play and the style of continuity distinctly separated these performances from the court ballets of the time; additionally, the comédies-ballets demanded that both the dancers and the actors play an important role in advancing the story. Intriguingly Louis XIV played the part of an Egyptian in 'Le Mariage forcé' (1664) and also appeared as Neptune and Apollo in his retirement performance of 'Les Amants magnifiques' (1670).

On 20th February 1662 Molière married Armande Béjart, whom he believed to be the sister of Madeleine. The same year he premiered 'L'École des Femmes' (The School for Wives), widely regarded as a masterpiece. It poked fun at the limited education given to daughters of rich families and reflected on Molière's own marriage. It attracted a lot of outraged criticism and ignited the protest called the "Quarrel of L'École des femmes". Molière responded with two works: 'La Critique de "L'École des femmes"', in which he imagined the audience of the previous work attending it. It mocks them by presenting them at dinner after watching the play; it addresses all the criticism raised about the piece by presenting the critics' arguments and then dismissing them. This was the so-called Guerre comique (War of Comedy), in which the opposite side was taken by writers like Donneau de Visé, Edmé Boursault, and Montfleury.

But more serious opposition was brewing, focusing on Molière's politics and his personal life. Some in French high society protested against Molière's excessive realism and irreverence, which were causing some embarrassment. Despite this the King expressed support for him. Molière was granted a pension and the King agreed to be the godfather of Molière's first son.

Molière's friendship with Jean-Baptiste Lully influenced him towards writing his 'Le Mariage forcé' and 'La Princesse d'Élide', written for royal divertissements at the Palace of Versailles.

'Tartuffe, ou L'Imposteur' was also performed at Versailles, in 1664, and created the greatest scandal of Molière's artistic career. Its depiction of the hypocrisy of the dominant classes was taken as an outrage and violently contested. It also aroused the wrath of the Jansenists (a Catholic theological movement, that emphasized original sin, human depravity, the necessity of divine grace, and predestination). The play was banned.

Molière was always careful not to attack the monarchy in any way. He had won a position as one of the king's favourites and enjoyed his protection from the attacks of the court. When the King suggested that Molière suspend performances of 'Tartuffe', Molière complied and quickly wrote 'Dom Juan ou le Festin de Pierre' (Don Juan, or, The Stone Banquet) to replace it. The story is of an atheist who becomes a religious hypocrite and is punished by God. But this too fell foul and was quickly suspended. The King, still keen to protect Molière became the new official sponsor of Molière's troupe.

With music by Lully, Molière presented 'Love Doctor or Medical Love'. The work was given "par ordre du Roi" (by order of the King) and was received much more warmly than its predecessors.

In 1666, 'Le Misanthrope' was produced. Molière's masterpiece. Although brimming with moral content it was little appreciated at the time and a commercial flop, forcing Molière to immediately write 'The Doctor Despite Himself', a satire against the official sciences. This was a success despite a moral treatise by the Prince of Conti, criticizing the theater in general and Molière in particular.

After the Mélicerte and the Pastorale comique, he tried again to perform a revised 'Tartuffe' in 1667, this time with the name of Panulphe or L'Imposteur. As soon as the King left Paris for a tour, the play was banned. The King finally imposed respect for 'Tartuffe' some years later, when he gained more power over the clergy.

Molière, now ill, wrote at a slower pace. 'Le Sicilien ou L'Amour peintre' (The Sicilian, or Love the Painter) was written for festivities at the castle of Saint-Germain-en-Laye, and was followed in 1668 by 'Amphitryon'.

'George Dandin, ou Le mari confondu' (The Confounded Husband) was little appreciated, but success returned with 'L'Avare' (The Miser), now very well known.

With Lully he again used music for 'Monsieur de Pourceaugnac', for 'Les Amants magnifiques' (The Magnificent Lovers), and finally for 'Le Bourgeois gentilhomme' (The Middle-Class Gentleman), another of his masterpieces. The collaboration with Lully ended with a tragédie et ballet, 'Psyché', written in collaboration with Pierre Corneille and Philippe Quinault.

In 1672, Madeleine Béjart died. It was a heavy blow to Molière who was already in declining health himself. However, he continued to write and his plays were eagerly awaited and performed. 'Les Fourberies de Scapin' (The Impostures of Scapin), a farce and a comedy in five acts was successful. The following play, 'La Comtesse d'Escarbagnas' (The Countess of Escarbagnas), is thought of as a lesser works.

'Les Femmes savantes' (The Learned Ladies) of 1672 is accepted as another masterpieces. It was born from the termination of the legal use of music in theater, (Lully had patented the opera in France and taken the best singers for his own works), so Molière returned to his traditional genre. It was a great success.

Molière suffered from pulmonary tuberculosis. One of the most famous moments in Molière's life was his last: he collapsed on stage in a fit of coughing and haemorrhaging while performing in the last play he'd written, in which, ironically, he was playing the hypochondriac Argan, in 'The Imaginary Invalid'.

Molière insisted on completing his performance.

Afterwards he collapsed again with another, larger haemorrhage and was taken home. Priests were sent for to administer the last rites. Two priests refused to visit. A third arrived too late. On 17th February 1673, Jean-Baptiste Poquelin, forever to be known as Molière, was pronounced dead in Paris. He was 51.

Under French law at the time, actors were forbidden to be buried in sacred ground. Molière's widow asked the King if Molière could be granted a normal funeral at night. The King agreed.

In his life Molière divided opinion. He was adored by the court and Parisians but loathed and reviled by moralists and the Catholic Church.

In 1792 his remains were brought to the museum of French monuments. In 1817 they were transferred to Père Lachaise Cemetery in Paris, close to those of La Fontaine.

In his 14 years in Paris, Molière singlehandedly wrote 31 of the 85 plays performed on his stage. His immensely popular legacy includes comedies, farces, tragicomedies and comédie-ballets.

Molière – A Concise Bibliography

Le Médecin Volant (1645)—The Flying Doctor
La Jalousie du Barbouillé (1650)—The Jealousy of le Barbouillé
L'Étourdi, ou le Contre-Temps(1653)—The Scatterbrain or The Bungler
L'Étourdi ou les Contretemps (1655)—The Blunderer, or, the Counterplots
Le Dépit Amoureux (16 December 1656)—The Love-Tiff
Le Docteur Amoureux (1658), 1st play performed by Molière's troupe (now lost)—The Doctor in Love
Les Précieuses Ridicules (1659)—The Affected Young Ladies
Sganarelle ou Le Cocu Imaginaire (1660)— Sganarelle or, The Self-Deceived Husband aka The Imaginary Cuckold
Dom Garcie de Navarre ou Le Prince Jaloux (1661)—Don Garcia of Navarre or the Jealous Prince
L'École des Maris (1661)—The School for Husbands
Les Fâcheux (17 August 1661)—The Mad aka The Bores
L'École des Femmes (1662; adapted into The Amorous Flea, 1964)—The School for Wives
La Jalousie du Gros-René (1663)—The Jealousy of Gros-René
La Critique de l'école des Femmes (1663)—Critique of the School for Wives
L'Impromptu de Versailles (1663)—The Versailles Impromptu
Le Mariage Forcé (1664)—The Forced Marriage
Gros-René, Petit Enfant (1664; now lost)—Gros-René, Small Child
La Princesse d'Élide (1664)—The Princess of Elid
Tartuffe ou L'Imposteur (1664)—Tartuffe, or, the Impostor
Dom Juan ou Le Festin de Pierre (1665)—Don Juan, or, The Stone Banquet (aka The Stone Guest, The Feast with the Statue)
L'Amour médecin (1665)—Love Is the Doctor aka Medical Love
Le Misanthrope ou L'Atrabilaire Amoureux (1666)—The Misanthrope, or, the Cantankerous Lover
Le Médecin Malgré Lui (1666)—The Physican in Spite of Himself aka A Doctor Despite Himself
Mélicerte (1666)
Pastorale Comique (1667)—Comic Pastoral
Le Sicilien ou L'Amour Peintre (1667)—The Sicilian, or Love the Painter
Amphitryon (1668)
George Dandin ou Le Mari Confondu (1668)—George Dandin, or, the Abashed Husband
L'Avare ou L'École du Mensonge (1668)—The Miser, or, the School for Lies
Monsieur de Pourceaugnac (1669)
Les Amants Magnifiques (1670)—The Magnificent Lovers
Le Bourgeois Gentilhomme (1670)—The Middle-Class Gentleman aka The Shopkeeper Turned Gentleman

Psyché (1671)—Psyche
Les Fourberies de Scapin (1671)—The Impostures of Scapin
La Comtesse d'Escarbagnas (1671)—The Countess of Escarbagnas
Les Femmes Savantes (1672)—The Learned Ladies aka The Learned Women
Le Malade Imaginaire (1673)—The Imaginary Invalid